❧

DINNER
IS
SERVED

❧

DINNER

IS

SERVED

AN ENGLISH BUTLER'S GUIDE
TO THE ART OF THE TABLE

by

Arthur Inch and Arlene Hirst

RUNNING PRESS
PHILADELPHIA · LONDON

Printed in United States

9 8 7 6 5 4 3
Digit on the right indicates the number of this printing

Library of Congress Control Number 2002095580

ISBN 0-7624-1558-4

Cover photography by Bill Jones
Cover design by Bill Jones
Interior design by Serrin Bodmer
Edited by Lynn Rosen
Typography: AGaramond and ATHandle Oldstyle

This book may be ordered by mail from the publisher.
Please include $2.50 for postage and handling.
But try your bookstore first!

Running Press Book Publishers
125 South Twenty-second Street
Philadelphia, Pennsylvania 19103-4399

Visit us on the web!
www.runningpress.com

CONTENTS

INTRODUCTION

There is no greater sight than a properly laid dinner table.
—ARTHUR INCH

Arthur Inch has seen, and set, quite a lot of dinner tables in his time. The eighty-seven-year-old retired butler spent over fifty years in private service in some of the noblest homes in Great Britain, a world known to most of us only from movies and television shows such as *Upstairs, Downstairs*, the famous PBS series. Mr. Inch lived in a world in which he tended people of great wealth and prestige, from Winston Churchill to the Queen Mother. Along the way, he has served the famous and the infamous, including Prince Rainier of Monaco, King Farouk, H.G. Wells, G.K. Chesterton, Anthony Eden, Generalissimo Franco, Neville Chamberlain and Queen Mary.

Because of his intimate knowledge of this long-ago time, Mr. Inch was enlisted by the producers of *Gosford Park*, Robert Altman's murder mystery of manners set in 1930s England, to be a technical adviser on the movie. It was he who explained to the filmmakers how things were actually done in these great homes, and he who helped ensure the film's authenticity.

Arthur Inch's career is part of a long tradition. The history of domestic service in England goes back to the Middle Ages, but it reached its apogee in Victorian times. By 1891, there were over one-and-a half million people toiling in the great estates and palaces; it was the second largest occupational group in the country. For Mr. Inch, private service was all in the family. His father managed to escape a life as a miner, choosing instead to begin his career as a hall boy to one of the local gentry. His mother, who came from a family of fourteen children, took her first job at the age of thirteen as the lowest ranked housemaid out of eight on an estate in Somerset. Mr. Inch also had six uncles and aunts who were in service, as well as a brother, who worked as Queen Elizabeth's chauffeur when Prince Charles was born.

Arthur Inch was born at Bishop's Hall in 1915, the youngest of three sons. What he remembers most vividly from his youth is the period that the family spent at Nidd Hall Estate in Yorkshire, a 109-room mansion sited on four thousand acres. (Today, it's a hotel.) Nidd Hall, like many country estates, was a small village unto itself. Efficiently run, almost self-supporting, the gardens produced all the flowers, fruits, and vegetables needed for the hall, and the surplus was

sold to a greengrocer and flower shop in nearby Harrogate. Servants were housed around the estate. Nidd Hall had an indoor staff of sixteen, which did not include the gardeners (of whom there were fourteen), chauffeurs, grooms, huntsmen, gamekeepers, and foresters, as well as a carpenter, blacksmith, plumber, painter, carter, and lorry driver. It was here that his father trained him for his life in private service.

Arthur Inch at the Spanish Embassy, with Phan, the ambassador's sheepdog.

In 1931, he left home for his first job: hall boy at Aldborough Hall, Boroughbridge, Yorkshire. It was a much smaller house than Nidd Hall. Here the indoor staff only numbered nine. And, at the tender age of fifteen he made his debut in the exalted position of butler, filling in for the actual butler on his half-day off every Wednesday.

At seventeen, he made the first of many career moves. "People were always coming and going from one job to another," he explains, "looking for a better job and earning promotions in rank along the way." He took the job of footman at West Wycombe Park,

Outside Alderborough Hall in Boroughbridge in Yorkshire.

Buckinghamshire (now one of the historic houses overseen by the National Trust). At that time, it was the residence of the premier baronet of Great Britain, Sir John Dashwood.

By the age of nineteen, Arthur Inch was the second footman of three at the Spanish Embassy in Belgrave Square. In his next post, he became first footman to the Duke of Marlborough at Blenheim Palace in Oxfordshire—an enormous establishment with an indoor staff of thirty-six. "The house was so big that the kitchen was a quarter mile away from the dining room," he remembers.

His next job was lady's footman at the Marquis of Londonderry's Park Lane House, where he was soon promoted to the job of under butler. The Marquis had five houses and used three of them. Not only was there an indoor staff of 36, there was a traveling staff and, in each of the three estates, a resident staff. He frequently worked twenty-hour days and, when he acquired a pedometer, discovered that he had walked eighteen miles in one house in one day. "Big houses had to be run like a ball of silk."

At Park Lane, he experienced what he calls the highlight of his life in private service: wearing the Marquis of Londonderry's state livery on the occasion of the coronation of King George VI, on May 12, 1937, which, he explains, qualified him to be called a "Knight of the Shoulder Knot." Full state livery included plush breeches, silk stockings, patent leather pumps with silver buckles, and an elaborate cutaway coat, covered with a mass of braid and crested silver buttons. From either the right- or left-hand shoulder were suspended the braided cords or loops ending in metal tags known as *aiglets*, familiarly called shoulder knots. All of this was crowned with an elaborate, powdered wig and a bicorne hat, making him look resplendent.

Another landmark in his life occurred during this period. In 1938 he met his future wife, Janet, who was working as a housemaid in the Marquis of Londonderry's country house in Mountstewart (about sixteen miles from Belfast, Ireland). The couple married in 1940 and had sixty-one years of happily married life before she died in February 2002.

When World War II broke out, Mr. Inch joined the Royal Air Force, where he became a fitter armourer—a military engineer—and worked on a spitfire squadron in Malta. During this time, his wife worked in a munitions factory. After the war, he tried out life as a civilian, working for a jeweler in Edinburgh. But the lack of advancement and housing shortages (a problem for a young married couple who by then had a small daughter, Elizabeth) lured him back into private service in 1956.

He worked as a butler in Norfolk and Reading before settling into a position at Heaselands in West Sussex, where he worked for the

Kleinwort family for twenty years. Here, instead of being one of ten menservants in a total staff of thirty-six, he was "a single-handed butler," meaning that he had to do a part of each of the ten men's jobs who worked in a large prewar establishment. He stayed on because the job was pensionable after ten years—a good thing for a family man—plus it provided a cottage on the grounds in which to live. "The future was quite good," he says. He retired at the age of sixty-five in 1980.

But Mr. Inch has not retired in the usual sense. For one thing, he has a passion for genealogy and has managed to fill ten file cabinets full of material that traces the roots of his family all the way back to the 1600s and to countries as far away as Australia. In addition, his keen memory and knowledge of English domestic history have led him to hold advisory roles. Besides acting as a technical consultant for *Gosford Park*, he also served in that capacity for an English television series, *The Edwardian Country House*, thus getting a chance to correct many of the errors about butlers that he had seen on other television programs. "They never dress them properly," he told the *Mid-Sussex*

Arthur Inch in full state livery for the coronation of King George VI in 1937.

Times, a local newspaper. "For example, at an evening dinner party, the butler dressed in white tie and tails, not black." (He did approve of the butler, Hudson's, garb in *Upstairs, Downstairs.* "He got it just about right," he says of that show's technical consultant.)

Arthur Inch has spent his entire career overseeing the production of beautiful dinners. "I do it properly, as it was done in the old days," he says. "The basics haven't changed. You just need someone to put it into practice." And now, with his expert guidance and insider secrets and tips, the art and elegance of a beautiful dinner table await you. So place your napkin on your lap, take your elbows off the table, and pull up a chair to a rich meal of cultural history and impeccable advice about the art of the table.

Arthur Inch at Bolnore, Haywards Heath, West Sussex in 1983.

PART I

———— ∞∞∞ ————

THE ESSENCE OF THE TABLE

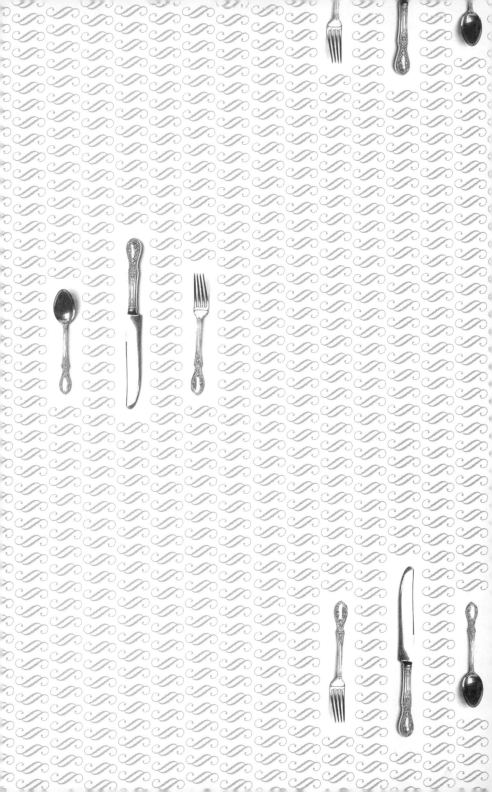

CHAPTER ONE

TABLE SETTINGS, THEN AND NOW

An elegant, formal dinner is one of the most joyous ways we have to commemorate special occasions, and a brilliantly set table makes all the difference. The key elements must all be in place—from the sparkling crystal and the perfectly polished silver to the fine translucent porcelain and impeccable linens. The atmosphere must be gracious and welcoming. Whether hosting or attending such an occasion, it's important to understand the basic traditions of serving dinners.

THE HISTORY OF FINE DINING

The ceremonies of fine dining have evolved over centuries. Formal entertaining, as we think of it today, has its roots in the Italian Renaissance, when wealthy merchants dined in high style. Catherine de Medici brought these customs with her to France in the mid-sixteenth century when she married the future king, Henry II. But it was during the reign of Louis XIV, the Sun King, from the mid-seventeenth century to the beginning of the eighteenth century, that the art of the table as we know it today was really born.

Under Louis XIV, dining table protocol was formally established. Dishes were served in a definite order and in containers designed especially for them. Forks became widely used, and matching sets of forks and spoons became common on affluent tables by the mid-eighteenth century. A host of European porcelain and glass factories sprang up.

It was also during this period that the dining room became a clearly defined space dedicated to one purpose: the service and enjoyment of food and all the pomp and circumstance that surround it.

Fine dining became (and still is) a key ingredient of French culture. During the Napoleonic era, Foreign Minister Talleyrand firmly believed that delicious meals presented at a graciously set table were unparalleled as a diplomatic tool.

THE VICTORIAN TABLE

The art of the table achieved its greatest heights of grandeur and extravagance in Victorian England, not coincidentally along with history's largest expansion in the manufacture of tableware. Mrs. Beeton, that era's arbiter of good housekeeping—and the Martha Stewart of her day—opined, "Dine we must, and we might as well dine elegantly as well as wholesomely."

The Victorians believed that every type of food required a special implement. But the excesses of the Victorian table—from chocolate spoons to eight different types of lettuce fork—were a middle-class phenomenon that the nobility ignored. For those who entertained in baronial splendor in the great houses of England, formal dinner parties adhered to a strict table-setting protocol. And, surprisingly enough, the basic rules haven't perceptibly changed since I worked with a thirty-six-person staff in the 1930s—there are just differences in scale and nuance. I shall now guide you through these seemingly complicated rules. They are simple, once you learn them.

PREPARING THE TABLE
THE FIRST STEPS

First, of course, comes the table. In Victorian, Edwardian, and Georgian times, it would be laid with a felt cloth to guard it from heat. This would then be covered with a lovely white damask cloth, with matching napkins finished to perfection in the house's own laundry. Later on, it became acceptable to use place mats.

If the table is to be bare, it must be well polished. In earlier days, we made up our own polish of beeswax and turpentine, which could produce a lustrous shine. To make this polish, we just melted a lump of beeswax down until it liquefied, then added turpentine and stirred the mixture until it became a thick paste. The hard part was the elbow grease we used while applying it! Nowadays, either a white cream polish or even spray polish is used. Whatever method you use, you must start with a well-polished table.

Next, find the center of the table, both lengthwise and crosswise, so that the centerpiece can be placed correctly. Then, as today, the centerpiece was usually floral. In the great houses, the flower arrangements would be done by the foreman gardener in the silver bowls and vases that would have been prepared for him. Sometimes, small silver trumpet-shaped vases were filled with a few low flowers to match the main arrangement. Long lengths of smilax fern would be entwined around the bowls of flowers as well as around the various silver spoons, birds, or cups placed symmetrically to finish off the center decoration.

A silver *epergne* (a type of centerpiece with a large central basin or basket with branches supporting candleholders and small baskets) was often used, and this center dish would have a selection of fruit arranged in the middle. Sometimes, flowers might be included in the small side vases, and chocolates and mints were placed in the small silver dishes in the *epergne*.

Candelabra were always used at formal dinners. Perhaps three nine-branch candelabra would be set along the length of the table, each fitted with white wax candles and special shade holders. (The shades were put on last after the candles had been lit.) For formal dinners today, try putting two or four candelabra at an equal distance from the center.

Today, these are no longer hard and fast rules, and a hostess has much more latitude when designing her centerpieces. The one rule that still applies is that everything must be geometrically spaced: The centerpiece must be in the actual center, the settings equidistant from each other, and all utensils balanced.

The most basic rule then and now is that there must be enough room for people to be at ease. Do not try to squeeze fourteen guests around a table designed for twelve. It would be uncomfortable for both the guests and the servers. Actual space between chairs depends on the size of the chair. A server should be able to get between them easily. There is no hard-and-fast rule because chairs vary in size. But there must be room for the servers to hand around the food or drinks. A rule of thumb for present-day hostesses is to allow two feet from the center of one setting to the center of the next.

SETTING THE TABLE

Once the centerpiece, candles, cloths or place mats, and chairs are in place, it was—and is—time to set the table. According to great house rituals, first comes the silverware, which must be perfectly aligned when it is placed at each guest's seat. For those setting tables today, most modern dining room tables have a band of different wood around the edge that provides a useful guide for placing the mats, knives, forks, and spoons.

The rule for setting out the cutlery (the English term for flatware) is to place the first-course utensils on the outside of the setting and then work your way inward for each subsequent course. So there might be a soup spoon on the extreme right, then a large table fork on the extreme left, which was used for the fish course. Next would come a table knife and fork for the meat course, followed by a spoon and fork for the pudding (never called dessert, as this term was reserved for fruit at the end of the meal). Finally, there would be a small knife and fork for the savory (a tangy dish traditionally served after sweets as a sort of palate cleanser). On the left-hand side would be a small side plate with a small butter spreader on it. Knife blades always face toward the plate. Today, an oyster or shellfish fork will be to the right of the soup spoon, or to the right of the knives, if soup is not being served. Of course, all the silver articles on the table would have been brightly polished previously and cotton gloves used to handle all the silver when placing it on the table. (See page 50 for the proper way to polish silver.)

If there were to be many courses at the dinner, we would only lay the table for soup, fish, and meat. (The same rule applies today.) Pudding spoons and forks would be placed on the table as soon as required—likewise, the knife and fork for the savories.

A FIVE-COURSE MEAL
(MORE OR LESS)

A dinner under five courses was hardly worth calling a dinner. Unlike today, there would be no service plate, or for that matter, any type of plate in front of the guest to start with. The folded napkin would be there, which the guests removed and placed in their lap, and then the first course would be served. If the first course were soup, it would be served from a side table from a soup tureen with a soup ladle, and placed in front of the guest. If the first course were to be fish, the server would place the empty plate in front of the guest and bring a platter to his left-hand side, and the guest would help himself or herself to whatever he or she required. The guests were never served their food directly by the server. That is hotel-style and not butler service.

Glasses on the table should be placed in a circle, starting with a sherry glass for the soup course, a white wineglass for the fish course, a claret (the English designation for French Bordeaux) or burgundy glass for the meat course, then a tumbler for water to rinse the palate, followed by a champagne glass for the pudding. Port, brandy, and liqueur glasses would be added later. The glasses must have first been washed in good soapy water, rinsed in hot water, and dried with a linen cloth.

In front of each guest, or between two, would be salt, pepper, and mustard. We would place silver ashtrays around the table with little miniature matchboxes in silver covers, although smoking wasn't allowed until after all the courses had been served, and then usually only by gentlemen after the ladies had withdrawn. Today, smoking is still taboo during the meal and, if your hostess has not put ashtrays on the table, she clearly doesn't want any smoking. Therefore, don't use your dessert plate or saucer as a substitute ashtray!

Name cards were typed (not handwritten, because typing made them more easily read by guests) and laid at each place. A plan of the table where duplicate cards could be inserted was to hand for her ladyship when she helped to seat the guests. Elaborate gilt-edged menu cards would also have been typed and put in menu-card holders and placed between diners so that they could see which dishes were coming and be able to decide which courses to pass or partake of, as there weren't many who chose every one.

CLEARING THE TABLE FOR A FINAL COURSE

After the savory course was finished, we had to clear the table. A footman would hold a large butler's tray, and the butler and valet would remove all the used glasses, and any knives, forks, spoons, toast racks, and condiment sets—except the salt, if nuts were to be served. The place mats would be removed and any crumbs brushed off with a special crumb brush and tray.

The fruit course would be served next. The setting for this consisted of one of the good china plates on which was placed a lace doily and on top of that a glass finger bowl with a small amount of water and perhaps a floating sprig of scented geranium leaf, or a flower. A silver gilt knife, fork, and spoon would be placed around the finger bowl and the whole ensemble then placed in front of each guest. The guest would then place the knife to the right, and the fork and spoon to the left side of the plate. When the fruit course was served, the guest would move the finger bowl to the upper left side of the dessert plate. Then the fruit would be served and when the guests had finished, they would dip their fingers into the bowls and dry them on napkins.

SERVING PORT

The phrase "pass the port" has two different meanings. In earlier days, the butler would pour a small amount of port into the host's glass. He would then taste it in front of his peers and pronounce it drinkable—proving that the wine had not been poisoned. Thus the host passed the port.

Its second meaning is less ominous. The butler first fills the host's glass and then proceeds clockwise around the table, filling the guests' glasses. When he finishes, he places the decanter in a wine coaster in front of the host and leaves the dining room. Then, when the glasses need topping up, guests ask the host to "pass the port." It travels clockwise around the table from guest to guest and back to the host.

My father taught me that the way to distinguish a good port from an inferior one is to pour a little in a glass, swirl it around the side and notice if the wine appears oily as it runs down. If it does, the port is quite satisfactory. (Today, we say it has legs.)

RETIRING TO THE DRAWING ROOM

After dessert, the hostess would signal to the ladies that they could retire to the drawing room for coffee. This room was originally known as the withdrawing room but it was eventually shortened to drawing room. The ladies would be served coffee and liqueurs there.

The gentlemen would then move up to the end of the table where the host would be sitting and would begin the ritual of passing the port. Brandy, cigars, and coffee would be served in the dining room.

Mr. Derisley, the butler at Aldborough Hall (the very first place I worked), believed that the silver coffeepot should never be washed out. When I went to clean it he would ask, "What has been in that pot?" Naturally, I would say, "Coffee." Then he would say, "Well, what's going into it?" and again the answer would be "Coffee." Whereupon he would gleefully remark, "Well, why wash it then?" And so the pot was never washed out. He claimed they got a stronger cup of coffee that way, and working, on the principle that coffee should be black as night, hot as hell, and sweet as a kiss, he was probably right.

In those times, the days were very long for the staff. The gentlemen would often sit in the dining room up till midnight before they left to join the ladies in the drawing room. Then the four tired menservants would have to clear the dining room and open all the windows to air the place. If a footman were on duty with either the butler, valet, or groom of chambers, he had to wait until all the gentlemen had retired so that he could clear the coffee cups and the grog tray and make sure all the log fires were damped down and old newspapers removed. This meant that we often had to work a twenty-hour day, from 6:30 A.M. right through to 2:30 the next morning. And then we had to start up again at 6:30 A.M. after only four hours of sleep!

❧ DECANTING WINES ❧

In my day, ports, clarets, and burgundies were all decanted in the wine cellar, never at the table.

Here are the rules I followed:

∞ Remove the bottle from its bin and carefully stand it upright.

∞ Using a double-handled corkscrew, gently remove the cork.

∞ Check the cork carefully to see if it is crumbly or musty. If it is, the wine will not be any good.

∞ Remove the black wax at the top of the bottle and brush off the bits, and then wipe off the neck of the bottle.

∞ Cover a wine funnel with a piece of muslin or cambric or a white handkerchief to filter the wine into the decanter.

∞ Tip the bottle slowly into the wine funnel.

∞ Place a lighted candle so it shines through the bottle and the sediment can be seen; do not stop decanting until the lees (sediment) reach the neck of the bottle.

∞ Check the wine to see if it is a nice bright color, and taste it to see if it is fit to drink.

∞ If it is port, put the decanter stopper in and take it to the dining room for tomorrow's dinner party. If it is claret or burgundy, use it the same day.

Today, wine at a formal dinner is opened in the kitchen, not at the table, and, if the wine needs decanting, the host may do it himself (as Sir Richard Kleinwort, my former employer, does), straining it with a paper coffee filter and big funnel. More frequently, wine, both white and red, is poured directly from the bottle, unless it is a vintage wine. The opened bottles may be kept on the sideboard, and when it is time for wine service, the butler takes the bottle, holding it in the palm of his hand with the label facing toward the guest so he or she may see the vintage. For chilled wines, a napkin is wrapped around the neck for insulation.

When pouring, to avoid spills, bring the bottle to the glass. When finished, twist the bottle over the glass to halt drips. When we served wine from the bottle, we would hold it in the right hand and have a small napkin in the left. After the wine was poured, we would hold the napkin under the neck of the bottle to catch any drips. The server should wipe the mouth of the bottle clean after pouring each glass if the bottle seems to be dripping. In my day, glasses were kept about three-quarters filled for both red and white wine. Today, wine enthusiasts recommend filling the glass a little less than half full, leaving enough space so that the wine can be gently swirled to release the wine's bouquet.

UPDATING THE TRADITION

That was how an elaborate dinner was served then, but nowadays it has to be much simpler, especially if you are doing it yourself. Very few people have large staffs to assist them! But a lovely table can still be achieved if one has time and patience. There's nothing like it if it is well done. The manners are the same. Only the style is different.

For one thing, remember to keep the meal simple. For example, you don't need to serve more than three courses, and avoid dishes that require intensive last-minute preparation—simple roasts or casseroles are easiest. And, although inappropriate for a true formal meal, the first course can be on the table before guests are called to dinner, and the water can be poured before the guests are seated. The main course can be assembled on individual plates in the kitchen, then brought to each guest, or the serving dishes can be placed on hot plates on the sideboard and guests can help themselves. (The word "buffet" means "sideboard" in French.) The host can pour the wine.

The basic rules for setting the table are exactly the same. Flatware for the first course should be on the outside of the setting and work its way inward for each subsequent course. There should never be more than three sets on the table. The bread and butter plate, with a small butter spreader on it, is still placed to the left of the setting. For large parties, name cards are still laid at each place, and menu cards are still used so that guests can pace themselves (and if your handwriting is illegible, you can generate them on a computer).

In the era of *Gosford Park*, the candles were always white, as were all of the table linens. But now, although I don't agree with this, just as it has on the tennis court, color has entered the picture. While I personally prefer the traditional settings, tablecloths in hues of blue, yellow, green, and pink are acceptable—an innovation brought about largely by Jacqueline Kennedy, according to Laetitia Baldrige, her former press secretary. And it was Mrs. Kennedy who broke the tradition of having guests sit at one long table; she found that round tables that seated just eight to ten people led to livelier conversation.

Another major difference between then and now is that women no longer withdraw to the drawing room after dinner, leaving the men to their port and cigars. The entire party leaves the dinner table at the same time, led by the hostess. But I must say that men have hated relinquishing this tradition!

Although many things have changed, I have kept up with the times. After I retired in 1980, I decided to put my experience as a butler to work, and I found that gradually I became a much wanted man (in the best sense) and in demand at luncheons, dinners, drinks, and even a breakfast party on New Year's Day. So for the last several years, my late wife, Janet (who died in 2002), and daughter, Elizabeth, have helped me with these parties at many, many houses in Sussex and Kent. I have enjoyed my contribution to the art of gracious living and hope to continue for a few more years yet!

⤙ BUILDING A BETTER ⤚ WINE CELLAR

If you are installing a wine cellar, these basic precepts still apply:

- A wine cellar should face north and be free from tremors.
- The cellar should be built at basement level, at least four yards below ground level and should ideally be excavated out of rock or chalk. The walls and bins should be brick-lined, then lime-washed. The floor is usually brick-lined.
- A saucer of water will show if any vibration is present. To make sure there are no drafts, hang a fine cloth from the ceiling and check to see that it doesn't move.
- If the room is damp, cover the floor with dry sand or use a small electric fire. Alternatively, if it is too dry, place a tray of wet sand on the floor to increase the humidity. The cellar will require two ventilators on different walls; one high up and one low down and not in line. Sometimes, holes were drilled in the door to supply more ventilation.
- Ideally, the temperature in the cellar should range from fifty-two to fifty-eight degrees Fahrenheit (eleven to fourteen degrees Celsius). If using a humidifier, set it at about sixty to seventy percent. Check for humidity by leaving a squeezed-out sponge on a plate: it should not have dried out after twelve hours.

- A cellar should be dimly lit using no more than a forty-watt bulb. Wine does not like ultraviolet light.
- Clear out any rubbish, and never store fruit, vegetables, or cheese there.
- To store wine, use the upper bins first. Lay bottles down horizontally to keep wine in contact with the cork, necks facing outward so that leakage can be easily observed.
- Label all of the bins and, if possible, use one bin for each type of wine, e.g. claret, burgundy, port, and white wine. If labels tend to come off (a sign of a damp cellar), a perfume-free lacquer can be applied to keep the labels on all bottles. (A splash of whitewash would be painted on top of the bottles in case the labels came off.) In modern times, of course, one can use wine cabinets that are thermostatically controlled and humidified.

NOTE: ALL CONVERSIONS IN THIS BOOK ARE APPROXIMATE.

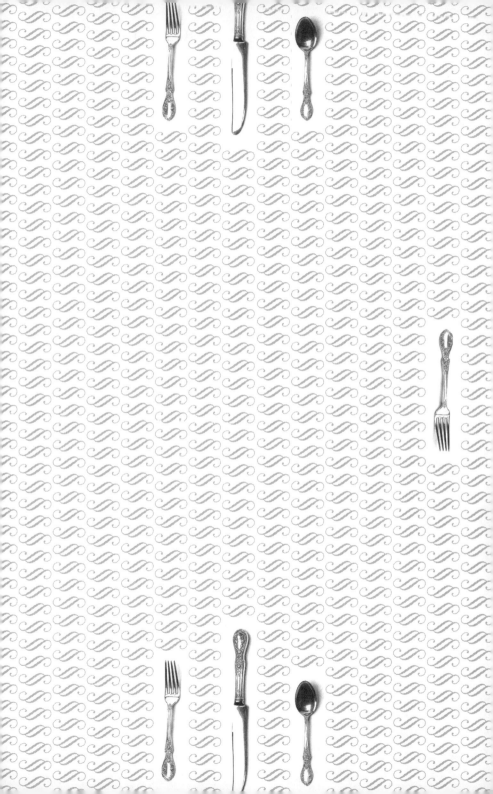

CHAPTER TWO

AT YOUR SERVICE

To prepare for a successful dinner party, I use the letters P. P.: planning and performance. I began this practice when I was just starting out as a lad of fifteen at Aldborough Hall in Yorkshire to help me avoid some of my mistakes.

For example, once whilst in the dining room I forgot to put the plates out on the table. When I took the main dish in my left hand and presented it to the lady to help herself, she very sarcastically asked me if she was supposed to put it on the place mat! It certainly impressed upon me never to make that mistake again. That's why P. P. is so important to me now.

Of course there are many things we used to do that unfortunately are not done any more. For one thing, before dinner, I used to take an instrument made of iron that had a cup at the end of a long handle and place it in the furnace fire until it was red hot. I'd then pour some liquid perfume into the red-hot cup and walk around the public rooms, spreading clouds of scented air, adding another touch of gracious living.

Alas, we shall never see the likes of those days in private service again! I feel privileged to have been a part of that scene, as I'm sure do many thousands of others who worked in similar places all over the British Isles. But, despite the disappearance of some charming customs, an elegant and proper dinner party can still be given. I have outlined below how a successful modern dinner party should proceed under the most ideal conditions. But even if you don't have ample staff, use the following as a general guide.

COCKTAILS

A manservant (today, it might be either a man or a woman server) is stationed at the front door to greet the guests when they arrive. He either takes their coats or directs them to a room where they can be left. There should be an envelope for each guest placed on a table in the entryway with the table number at which the guest is to be seated (if there are several tables). At large formal dinners, there should also be a table chart, propped up with the help of an easel back, in plain sight.

After a guest has been greeted by the hostess, a waiter should then ask that person, "May I get you a drink?" During cocktail hour, the staff's job is to supervise the drink service, replenishing glasses and seeing that no one is lacking for hors d'oeuvres. If there are smokers, the staff empties ashtrays when necessary. Before dinner is announced, the butler (or a designated waiter) lights the candles in the dining room and fills the water glasses. When the butler announces that dinner is served, the host and hostess collect the guests of honor and proceed into the dining room. The host and the honored woman guest enter first, the hostess last. Each man is expected to seat the woman on his right. If a woman arrives before anyone else, she may seat herself, although if there is a waiter nearby, he will probably rush to seat her. All the women should be seated before the men sit down.

THE DINNER

At a very big formal dinner served by a large staff, the butler stands behind the hostess's chair, except when managing his staff or pouring wine. His duty is to see that everything goes smoothly, and he is not supposed to leave the dining room. (He only serves food if there is not enough additional staff to do the serving, and then only the main course.) At a smaller dinner, the butler does everything himself, or else he'll serve the main course, and a waiter will follow him with accompanying dishes or vegetables. But whether there are four people at a table or twenty-four, the service of the meal proceeds in exactly the same sequence and manner.

The basic rule is to serve food from the left and drinks from the right. As for the order in which guests are served, always start with the lady guest sitting to the right of the host, and continue clockwise. I disapprove of the custom of serving all the ladies before serving the gentlemen. There is nothing worse than dodging around. The male guest to the right of the female guest of honor will be the last to be served. He is in what is known as "Starvation Corner." Hopefully he partook of the *hors d'oeuvres!*

SERVING THE MAIN COURSE

One of the main changes in formal table setting is the use of service plates. In my days of private service, service plates were not used. I don't understand why, but modern etiquette books seem to universally decree that there should never be an empty space in front of a guest. (The only exception to this rule is when the table is cleared for dessert.) It is contemporary practice to have service plates laid on the table before the guests enter the dining room. But I still prefer to do without them.

At some dinners, the first course may already be on the table when the guests enter the dining room. It may be in a stemmed glass or in a bowl on top of a plate, which sits atop the service plate. When this course is finished, the entire unit is cleared, but the place plate remains. The soup course is served next. When the guest is finished, the place plate and soup plate are removed together, and a warm plate for the fish course, if there is one, or a heated dinner plate for the main course should immediately be substituted.

If the dinner party is a large one, it is necessary to have serving dishes presented simultaneously to each group of six or eight guests. This ensures that guests eat at the same time and that hot foods will be properly hot. If there are two servers going around the table, the second server begins with the man to the right of the hostess.

During the period that I worked at Blenheim Palace, the food was brought to the dining room course by course from the kitchen, which was almost a quarter of a mile away. We had to move quickly to keep the dishes hot! I believe that an earlier Duke of Marlborough had complained that he had never had a hot meal at Blenheim, as by the time the dishes arrived in the dining room, they were already cold.

Today, a waiter brings one plate at a time to the table and serves each guest from the left. When guests have finished that course, he removes the plates one at a time with his left hand, never piling one on top of the other. When all the plates have been removed, the plates for the next course are brought to the table. Guests are served one at a time.

To expedite the first course, a waiter carries two plates to the table at one time. Standing between two guests, he places the plate in his left hand in front of the guest on his left and the plate in his right hand in front of the guest on his right. He removes the plates exactly the same way when the course is finished. When it's time to serve dessert, the same procedure gets repeated.

The waiter will pass dinner rolls in a shallow serving dish or basket lined with a napkin. After vegetables, bread, and condiments are passed, they should be returned to the sideboard or the kitchen. The waiter removes utensils used for a course along with the spent dishes for that course. If a guest has mistakenly used the wrong fork or knife, the server should clear them without comment, along with the ones that should have been used, and replace them with the appropriate clean ones for the next course.

The waiter makes sure that all the guests have finished eating before removing plates, with one exception. In the case of a noticeably slow eater, the waiter can start removing plates as unobtrusively as possible and return to the slow eater at the end.

Waiters always pass a serving platter with the left hand, steadying it, if necessary, with the right. A second waiter, who follows immediately, passes sauces or gravies. Ladles for the sauce should be in the sauce when it is served, and the bowl or boat should be on a silver salver, or tray, that is lined with a paper doily. Sauces can be served separately in a sauceboat or to the left of the meat or fish on the serving platter.

When serving hot food, the waiter places a napkin under the serving dish to provide insulation for his hand. The dish should be held in the left hand and served from the left side of the guest. The right hand should be held behind one's back and never in any circumstances should it be allowed to rest on the chair back. The serving fork and spoon are placed facedown on the serving platter or vegetable dish with the handles facing in the direction of the guest.

All serving dishes should be held at a comfortable level—about one inch above the guest's plate—not too high or so far away that guests have to twist around to reach them. To avoid spills and provide easy access to the platter, the waiter should hold it partially over the table in a level position. The proper way to remove a platter is to raise it above the guest's shoulder.

When I was in the employ of the Spanish Embassy, after we had served a course and the guests were eating, we had to stand in the four corners of the room absolutely still with an expressionless face and pretend we were deaf to all the conversation going around.

THE DESSERT SERVICE

After guests have finished the main course, the first things to be removed from the table are any platters or serving dishes. Then the dinner plates are cleared, along with the flatware. The last things to be taken away are smaller plates, bread plates, and finger bowls. In the United States at formal dinners, salad is served after the main course. Before dessert is served, a waiter will remove the unused flatware and place it on a small tray. Only glasses should remain on the table (and, of course, the centerpiece and other decorations). The server then crumbs the table, using a folded napkin and, from the left of each place setting, brushes any crumbs onto a small tray, a clean plate, or silent butler (a lidded, hinged receptacle with a short handle). Before dessert is served, all traces of earlier courses must be removed. A good way to remember: the word dessert comes from the French *desservir*—to clear the table. No one likes to stare at the remnants of a meal.

THE MODERN WAITER'S DO'S AND DON'T'S OF FORMAL DINING

- In the great houses the butler carved the meat at the serving table in the dining room. Today, it seems that meat is carved in the kitchen or pantry, not at the table.
- Individual service requires two hands.
- Serve each course at the proper temperature.
- Second helpings are not offered. They are not necessary at a five- or six-course meal.
- Courses should follow in an unbroken rhythm. Passing of crackers, breads, and relishes, and refilling of water glasses takes place during, not between, the appropriate courses.
- Good service is quiet and unobtrusive, so waiters must avoid noises that disrupt conversation and handle utensils carefully and silently. Waiters should never stop abruptly.
- Flatware, glasses, cups, and saucers are always carried on a tray, never in a waiter's hands. And for safety and to prevent clattering, the trays should be covered with a napkin.
- Always carry a stack of plates with both hands. Plates should be wrapped in a towel so that they are not touched with bare hands.
- A piece of cake or pie should be served with the point facing the guest.

LEFT AND RIGHT RULES

To the Guest's Left Side

- Present platters.
- Hold the platter when guests help themselves.
- Serve salad when it is served as a side dish.
- Serve bread for the bread plates.
- Clean the table of breadcrumbs with a folded napkin or crumber.

To the Guest's Right Side

- Set and clear plates.
- Replenish or change flatware.
- Pour beverages and present wine bottles.

SERVING WINE

- Glasses are placed in order of their use, above the knives.
- Wine, water, and champagne glasses are filled without lifting the glass from the table.
- To prevent dripping, a napkin is wrapped loosely around the neck of a champagne or wine bottle with the label exposed.
- All glasses are always placed to the right of the guest with the right hand. Beverages are always poured from the right side of the guest.
- When serving heavy red wines that have been decanted or are in a wine basket, hold the glass slightly slanted on the table with the left hand, and slowly pour the wine with the right hand so that the sediment is not disturbed. (In my time, the wine would have been decanted and sediment cleaned before serving.)

∽ If a white wine is served with an appetizer, the empty glasses are removed only after the red wine has been poured.

∽ Glasses can stay in place throughout the meal or be removed after a particular wine is no longer being served.

SERVING COFFEE

After-dinner coffee may be served at the table or in the living room. If it is at the table, the waiter brings in demitasse cups and saucers on a silver tray and places them to the guest's right. A second waiter follows with the coffeepot (or pots, if both regular and decaffeinated are being offered), cream, and sugar. Another way to serve is to place already filled demitasse cups and saucers to the right of the guests. A second waiter passes the cream and sugar. Chocolates, mints, or other candies are passed just after coffee has been served. Demitasse cups and saucers are not removed until the guests have left the table.

If coffee is served in the living room, while the guests are at dinner, one of the waiters should have straightened up, removed cocktail glasses, emptied ashtrays, and plumped up pillows. When guests return to the living room, a waiter brings unfilled demitasse cups and saucers, sugar, and cream into the room on a tray. A second waiter follows him with the coffeepot (or pots). The second waiter takes a cup and saucer from the first waiter's tray and fills it, handing one to each guest, and the guest helps himself to cream and sugar. A waiter may also bring in cups that are already filled on a tray from which guests may serve themselves. Another, less formal option is to place the coffee tray on a table in front of the hostess, who then pours the coffee. She will hand the cup and saucer to the waiter who takes it to a guest on a tray, along with cream and sugar.

After coffee has been served, liqueurs are passed, with the waiter asking each guest his or her preference. Sometimes a tray with glasses and liqueurs is set up on a table in the living room and the host offers and pours them. The host or hostess should have arranged with the butler beforehand what time the staff can depart. It's usually wise to have at least one waiter stay until all the guests have left.

⁂

Good service enhances a meal, as I well know from my many years of experience. Serve with style, and an elegant dinner party is assured!

PART II

———— ∞∞∞ ————

THE TOOLS OF THE TABLE

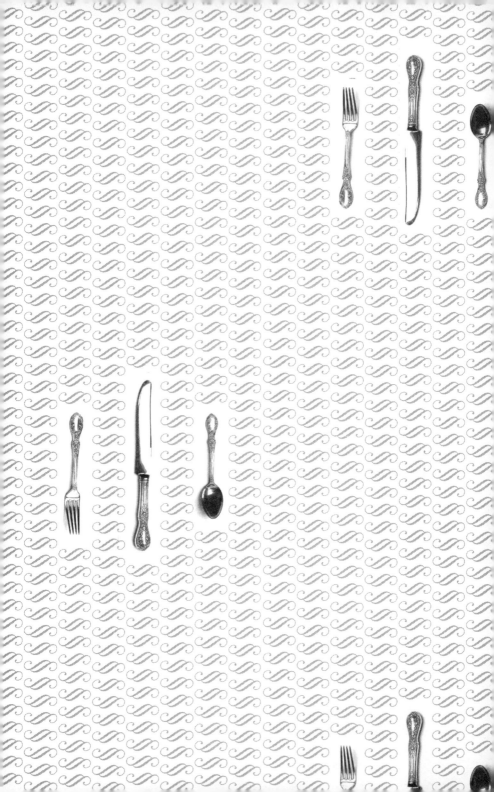

CHAPTER THREE

KNIVES, FORKS, AND SPOONS

Historically, precious metals have always connoted wealth, and silver dinnerware was a way to flaunt it. In my time, the family silver was so precious it was kept in special vaults. It was like going into Aladdin's cave to see the light reflected off all the polished silver. All around the walls would be green-baize-covered shelves, stacked with the silver that was in current use—the 1,001 pieces that went into making up a dining table and meant such a lot to gracious living.

Large silver chests on the floor were used to store the large pieces of plate. They were customized to fit each individual piece and to keep the silver from tarnishing, as the atmosphere couldn't penetrate. These chests were iron banded, had strong locks, and could, if necessary, be transported from house to house. A very heavy safe door would protect all this treasure, and when it was bolted and locked, the under butler would sleep with the key under his pillow. I believe that in some places, years ago, his bed was the sort that pulled down out of a cupboard and stretched completely across the safe door so it would be impossible for a burglar to get to the safe without awakening the under butler.

Even today, of all the tableware selections you'll make, the one that is most likely to become a future heirloom is your silver. It will not only endure, it will gain in beauty as it ages.

When people refer to silver, they usually mean hallmarked sterling silver. Sterling silver is made of 92.5 percent pure silver and 7.5 percent of a base metal, usually copper. The European mark for sterling is 925 (i.e., 92.5 percent pure silver). The reason sterling is not one hundred percent silver is that the pure metal is too soft for practical purposes and must be alloyed with other metals to give it the strength and hardness necessary for use. In the United States, federal law governs the formula, and anything sold as sterling silver must contain the prescribed amounts.

OTHER TYPES OF "SILVERWARE"

People frequently employ the term "silverware" to mean all utensils used for eating, but the correct word is "flatware" (in England, the word "cutlery" is used), which encompasses all kinds of metal—sterling, silver plate, and stainless steel.

SILVER PLATE

This is silver that is only skin deep. It is made by electroplating a layer of silver to a base metal—usually an alloy of nickel, copper, and zinc. A bar of base alloy is dipped into a big tub of water; silver bars are added, then acid, and an electric current is passed through which ionizes the silver molecules. These are then conducted to the base metal. The quality of silverplate depends mainly on the amount of silver used and the type and thickness of the base metal. To be assured of quality, look for the name of a reputable manufacturer. Silver plate may be used at formal dinners.

❧ POLISHING SILVER ❧ THE TRADITIONAL WAY

It used to be the footman's job to clean the silver. He would use Goddard's plate powder mixed with Scrubs cloudy ammonia (both products are still available today) for everyday cleaning, but if he had time, he would work with jeweler's rouge. This is a very fine red powder that was mixed with plain water to create a creamy consistency and then rubbed on the silver with either a silver rubber, a piece of box cloth, or bare fingers. If it was done long enough, it produced a brilliant luster on the silver as well as giving it a rich, dark color. The rubbers, which were oblong pieces of a type of sponge, were used to get into awkward corners. Squares of livery box cloth were also used to do the really hard rubbing. But it was always finished off with rubbing by the bare hands or fingertips.

When the rouging was complete, the silver would be washed out using a lather of soda and soft soap, then rinsed in hot water, dried with a fine linen cloth, and, finally, gently rubbed over with a thick chamois leather to remove any smears.

❧ ARTHUR INCH'S ❧ MODERN RECIPE FOR CLEANING SILVER

Ingredients

Goddard's Silver Dip

Goddard's Long Term Silver Polish

Long Term Silver Polishing Cloths (blue)

Two good, thick, large, soft chamois leathers (these should
never be washed)

Material

Cotton gloves for handling silver

Two plastic bowls (for use with Silver Dip and washing up)

Foam rubber sponges

Dishwashing detergent

Soft drying cloths

Soft-bristled brushes

Method

If the silver is tarnished, put some Silver Dip into a plastic
bowl, then sponge and brush it over the article until all the
tarnish is removed. Rinse it off in a separate bowl of hot water
and dry it off. Next, apply the Long Term Silver Polish with a
piece of foam rubber sponge and rub it well into the article for
a few minutes, then allow it to dry. (Articles that are chased,
i.e., engraved or etched, will need a soft brush to whisk the
polish into the intricate parts.)

Finally, brush off the dry powder and finish the piece with the Long Term Silver Polishing Cloths. If the article is very elaborately chased, it can be washed out in dishwashing liquid, then dried and polished with the silver cloths. Note: Don't allow Silver Dip to come into contact with stainless steel, as it will mark it and the stains are very difficult to remove.

STAINLESS STEEL

An alloy of three metals—chromium, nickel, and steel—stainless steel was born in the twentieth century, a product of the rapidly advancing technology that came out of World War II. It is extremely durable, dishwasher-safe and resists all kinds of staining. (Stainless means without stain; i.e., it will only stain under extreme conditions.) As with silver plate, there are many grades on the market. The highest quality stainless steel will be marked 18/10; that means eighteen percent chromium and ten percent nickel have been added to the basic steel alloy. Stainless steel is never used at formal settings.

When it comes time to select your flatware, do consider buying hallmarked sterling. Many people no longer want to be bothered with cleaning and polishing silver, but it is an essential element in gracious dining and, for me, it is well worth the bother.

GENERAL GUIDELINES

Dishwashers are not sterling-silver friendly. The vibrations subject the soft metal to scratches, and water spots leave marks that can etch the surface. Moreover, the heat of the machine tends to soften the metal. Wash silver by hand in hot sudsy water as soon as possible after using it, then give it a hot rinse. Dry it immediately. Don't use a detergent with bleach, which destroys the beautiful patina that provides much of sterling's aesthetic value.

The best way to care for sterling silver is to use it all the time. The more it is used, the more beautiful it becomes. This seeming paradox is true because a patina forms on the metal when it is constantly exposed to the air. A patina is a fine film resulting from the oxidation of silver with the air. It usually develops in all of the little scratches that occur with daily usage. A patina gives silver a lustrous, mellow finish.

To retard tarnish, keep silver away from heat and sunlight as well as salt, sulphur, or gas fumes, and never place it in direct contact with rubber.

Rotate the pieces of your sterling service. You most likely will not be using your complete set every day, so when you use any of it, the patina and wear should be evenly distributed. If you don't rotate your flatware, some pieces will look like heirlooms and some will look as if they have just come out of their plastic bags from the store.

Pacific cloth, a tarnish-preventing material made of cotton flannel embedded with tiny particles of pure silver, repels tarnish-making gases. It is used as a liner in most silver chests. It can be purchased in most yard goods stores and some silver departments. Some Americans claim that if you line the drawer in which you keep your silver with this fabric you don't need to have a separate silver chest, but I've never done this.

FLATWARE OR CUTLERY

When you shop for flatware or cutlery today, the price is usually quoted by the six-piece place setting, which consists of a teaspoon, soup spoon, salad fork, butter spreader, knife, and fork (you will often find five-piece place settings as well where the butter spreader has been omitted). Knives and forks are available in three sizes: luncheon, place, and dinner. Dinner knives and forks are about three quarters of an inch (eight centimeters) longer than place size, while the luncheon size is about a half inch smaller than place. The prices given for a place setting are usually for the place size.

Dinner-size flatware is sometimes referred to as "continental size." In my day, the place category was unknown. It was basically made for the American market, which found the larger size cumbersome. In recent years the larger size has risen in popularity and looks majestic at a formal table. Also, soup spoons didn't make an appearance on English upper-class tables until after World War II. They used large serving spoons instead.

ADDITIONAL FLATWARE

You may have need for other specialized pieces throughout the meal. Some of these include:

Spoons

The word comes from the Anglo-Saxon *spon* which means "splinter" or "chip," because the first spoons were carved from wood.

Cream Soup

This spoon has a round bowl specially designed to dip into cream soup bowls, which are round and deep. Since cream soups are rarely served at formal dinners (cream soup is too rich for a multicourse meal), they are not essential to own for those occasions.

Bouillon
Smaller than the cream soup but similar in shape; its use is very specialized.

Citrus
Used when serving grapefruit, orange, or other citrus fruits, its sharply pointed tip makes it very helpful for digging out sectioned segments.

Iced Beverage
Also known as an iced teaspoon, these are very popular in warm climates, for example in the southern United States. We traditionally never used them.

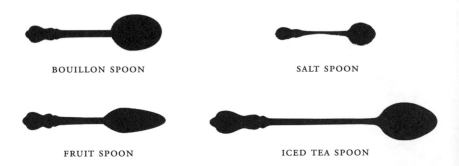

BOUILLON SPOON   SALT SPOON

FRUIT SPOON   ICED TEA SPOON

In fact, contrary to commonly held notions of long gone baronial splendor, all the spoons noted above were unknown in England's great houses. The ones following, however, were employed.

Individual Salt
Designed for use with open salt dishes, also known as salt cellars, their bowls are usually gilded, i.e., gold-plated, because salt corrodes silver.

After-Dinner Coffee

Also called a demitasse, it is used most frequently at formal dinner parties, just as it was in pre-World War II England.

KNIVES AND FORKS

Cocktail Fork

This is used for all types of shellfish and also for hors d'oeuvres.

Fish Knife and Fork

These were introduced around 1850, but, as I mentioned above, they were considered to be middle class. However, they have gained favor because of their usefulness, and for providing more leverage for separating the meat of the fish from the bones.

OYSTER/COCKTAIL FORK

FISH FORK

ICE CREAM FORK

FISH KNIFE

Individual Steak Knife

A specialized knife that is usually not part of a flatware pattern. (In the houses of the nobility, it was not used prior to World War II.)

Ice Cream Fork or Spoon

Both of these utensils were designed for cold desserts. Neither is correct to use at formal dinner parties—two utensils, a dessert fork and dessert spoon, are provided instead.

There now exists a host of other specialized utensils, most of which originated during Victorian times. These range from five o'clock teaspoons to chocolate spoons, fruit knives and forks, pastry forks, strawberry forks, and specialized forks for lobsters, snails, and oysters. None of these are used at formal tables.

SERVING PIECES

It is also very important to have just the right serving pieces. So many beautiful pieces are designed for specialized uses, and each dish should have its own.

Carving Set

These are available in two sizes: steak (small) and roast. They usually come with a sharpening steel to hone the cutting blades.

Cold Meat or Serving Fork

A large fork used to serve sliced meat, chops, and a variety of salads.

Ladles

Ladles come in many sizes: punch, soup, gravy, cream, and mustard, to name the most common. The size you will need depends on what you are serving. The proportion of the ladle should match that of the container.

Lemon and Olive Forks

The major difference between a lemon fork and an olive or pickle fork is that the lemon fork has three tines; an olive has only two.

CITRUS (LEMON) FORK   SUGAR SPOON

GRAVY LADLE   SUGAR TONGS

Pastry Server
With its blade, it's an indispensable tool for pies and cakes as well as frozen desserts.

Pierced Serving Spoon
For any fruit or vegetable that is served in its own juices.

Sugar Spoon
The implement for dispensing granulated sugar, the form in which sugar is most commonly served today.

Sugar Tongs
The correct utensil for cubed sugar, which some deem the only proper way to serve sugar at a formal meal.

Table or Serving Spoon
One of the most basic utensils for vegetables, salads, fruits, and all manner of desserts.

All of the serving utensils listed below, while well-known today, were not used by families in the homes where I was employed.

Bonbon or Nut Spoon
Designed to serve candy or nuts at the tea table. Its bowl can be solid or pierced.

Butter Knife
Not to be confused with individual butter spreaders, which are smaller, it's used only at informal meals, not at formal events.

Cheese Serving Knife
Most flatware patterns today come with an all-purpose tool with a wide flat blade. However, there are several types of cheese knives: cleavers for hard cheese; planes for slicing hard and semi-hard cheeses; triangular, wedge-shaped blades for soft cheeses; and knives with serrated, curved tips to lift sliced cheese to the plate.

Jelly Server
Specifically designed for molded jelly dishes such as aspics.

Tomato or Flat Server
It is useful for tomatoes, cucumbers, eggs, asparagus, or salads, but a serving spoon and fork are usually sufficient for these tasks.

At a formal dinner, it is not necessary that all the silver match, although all forks or all spoons or all knives should be of the same pattern at one place setting. Dessert silver, which is not on the table but is brought in with the dessert plates at a formal dinner, need not match the dinner service. After-dinner coffee spoons can also be a totally different pattern.

Remember, having just the right serving piece or utensil for each dish will give your table the perfect touch.

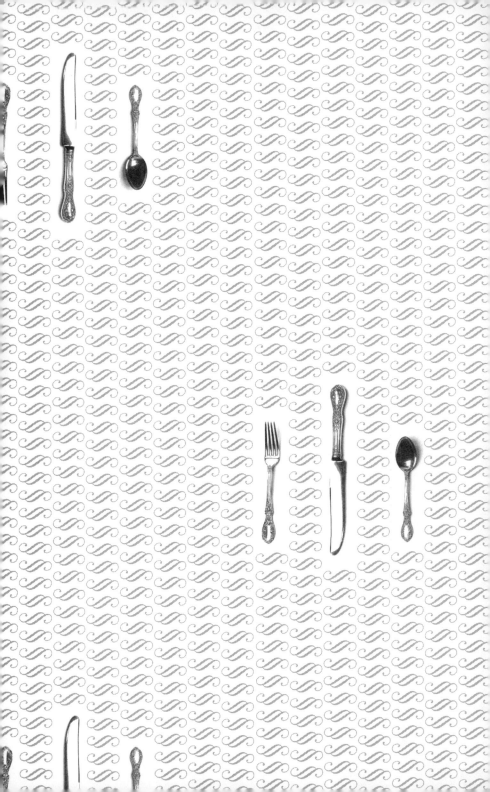

CHAPTER FOUR

PLATES, CUPS, AND SAUCERS

I n the time of England's great houses, fine china played second
fiddle to silver at the table, because all the dinner plates were sterling. In these large establishments, the soup, fish, and meat plates
were solid hallmarked silver with the master's crest, and when placing
the plate on the table, we had to make sure that the crest was at the
top. (Today, the same rule applies: If a plate has a figural pattern it
must be placed so that the figure faces the diner.) Just imagine what a
glittering table was set with all that silver! And what a big investment,
which, sadly, most people can't afford today.

In today's world, china has replaced silver as the most important
element on the table, and, unfortunately, sterling silver dinner plates
have gone the way of England's great estates. Now it is the dinnerware
pattern that commands the viewers' eyes immediately, creating the
mood as well as conveying the hosts' own sense of style.

The word "china" is commonly employed as a general term to
describe all kinds of dinnerware, but there are really several different
kinds, most of which are ceramic, i.e., made from clay. But it is fine
china, or porcelain, that is used at formal dinners. (And, contrary to
what most people think, porcelain is much more durable and practical for daily use than earthenware, which has a softer body.)

When shopping for fine dinnerware, note that it is traditionally
priced by the place setting, which typically includes five pieces: dinner

plate, salad plate, bread and butter plate, and teacup and saucer. But while it is priced as a complete setting, you don't have to purchase it this way. For example, you may want to purchase a dessert service in a completely different pattern.

MATERIAL DIFFERENCES IN DINNERWARE

PORCELAIN

This is made from a combination of clays—kaolin, quartz, and feldspar—that is fired at a very high temperature to make the body extremely hard. Porcelain is nonporous, smooth, and translucent because the high firing has made it vitrified—literally, glass-like. If you hold a porcelain plate to the light and pass your hand behind it, you'll see its shadow. Some of the most famous makers of porcelain include Rosenthal, Lenox, Noritake, and of course, all the French manufacturers from the town of Limoges, France. (By the way, Limoges is a place, not a factory!)

BONE CHINA

This is a type of porcelain that contains animal ash (usually ox bone) or a chemical equivalent to whiten it. There is no difference in quality between porcelain and bone china. The distinction is in the color of the body. Bone china is a creamy white; porcelain has a more grayish cast. Both are considered fine china. English potters invented bone china, and English manufacturers are in the forefront of producers today: Wedgwood, Royal Crown Derby, Royal Doulton, Minton, and

Spode are just a few of the famous brands.

The large, stately homes in which I was employed had fine china from many of the well-known factories in the U.K. (some of which no longer exist)—from Bow, Chelsea, Derby, Longton Hall, Worcester, Bristol, Coalport, Minton, Rockingham, and Wedgwood. They also had porcelain from the continent—Sevres from France and Meissen from Germany. These all had their individual marks on their bases, which was very useful for identifying the factories and often dating them as well. Usually these sets were kept in glass-fronted cabinets spaced around the room.

❧ WOMEN'S WORK ❧

Traditionally, only the menservants dealt with the silver. The women servants looked after the porcelain. The pudding and savory plates would be chosen from various well-known makers such as Sevres, Chelsea, Crown Derby, and Rockingham, and these various sets were kept in a special china room and looked after by the housekeeper. She and the head housemaid would wash and dry them after use and put them back in the display cabinets along with the fruit dishes of the various patterns.

EARTHENWARE

Made from heavier, less refined clays, earthenware is fired at much lower temperatures, making it possible to produce very strong, bright colors—FiestaWare is a good example. Earthenware is slightly porous and is not as strong as fine china. It's opaque: The shadow of your hand will not be visible if you hold it up to the light.

STONEWARE

The link between earthenware and china, stoneware is usually semi-vitrified. In appearance, it seems very much like earthenware with its heavier weight and earthy colored body; in strength and durability, however, it's much closer to china. Neither earthenware nor stoneware is used at a formal dinner. Some of the best-known stoneware comes from the Arabia factory in Finland.

The biggest problem that people face today is deciding among all the options that are available to them. The choices are mind-boggling. The best advice is to use the way you live as a guide. If you hate the idea of washing things by hand, then you must buy things that are labeled dishwasher-safe. If convenience is of the utmost importance, choose a pattern that is ovenproof and microwave proof. But whatever you select, make the most of what you have. Remember that colors, glazes, and textures add excitement to the table.

ADDITIONAL PIECES

PLATES

The sizes of plates keep changing as dining habits change. In my day, multicourse meals were common, and a number of smaller plates were needed. These days, there are a variety of sizes, large and small.

Service Plate

Generous in size—it ranges from twelve to fourteen inches (thirty-one to thirty-six centimeters) in diameter—a service plate is also known as a charger or buffet plate. When used at a formal setting today, it is removed from the table after the guests are seated. It is never used under a dinner plate. It can also be used as a liner to create interesting contrasts in informal settings. Service plates were never used in my time.

Luncheon Plates

Eight-and-a-half inches to nine-and-a-half inches (twenty-two to twenty-four centimeters) in diameter, these were de rigueur at teatime in the days of George VI, but they were not used for formal dinners. Today, they are not always available in every pattern and are never included in prepackaged sets.

BOWLS

Before World War II, no bowls of any sort were used. Instead, there was a succession of various-sized plates. But now there is a wide variety of bowl shapes and sizes from which to choose.

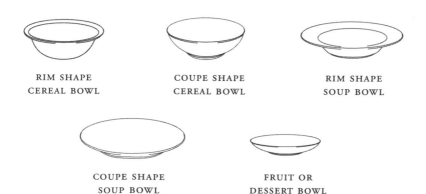

RIM SHAPE
CEREAL BOWL

COUPE SHAPE
CEREAL BOWL

RIM SHAPE
SOUP BOWL

COUPE SHAPE
SOUP BOWL

FRUIT OR
DESSERT BOWL

Rim Soup

This is the correctly sized bowl for formal dinners. In informal settings it can, of course, be used for pastas, risottos, or stews.

Coupe Soup

This more modern shape comes in all coupe-shaped (i.e. rimless) dinnerware designs. If your formal pattern is coupe-shaped, then this would be appropriate for formal dining.

Cream Soup Cup and Stand

The cup has two handles—one on either side—is footed, and rests in the well of a saucer (or "stand," as it is called). There are also bouillon cups and stands, which are smaller versions of the cream soup. Neither cream nor bouillon cups and stands are used at formal meals.

Cereal or Oatmeal

These extremely versatile dishes are also good in less formal settings, for cereals, soups, salads, and desserts.

Fruit Dish

A scaled-down version of the oatmeal (it has the same profile), this is the true dessert-service size.

Cups

After-Dinner Cup and Saucer

Popularly called a demitasse (which translates as half cup), this size is popular today with espresso drinkers.

Breakfast Cup and Saucer

Larger than the seven- or eight-ounce (207 to 237 milliliters) teacup and saucer (its capacity ranges from twelve to fourteen ounces or 355 to 414 milliliters), it is the size for people who need large infusions of caffeine in the morning.

CUP & SAUCER   CUP & SAUCER   AFTER DINNER
(FOOTED)   (FLAT)   MUG   CUP & SAUCER

MUGS

In our contemporary world, these are in such popular demand that they are offered in many fine china patterns and frequently outsell teacups and saucers. Though mugs certainly existed in early twentieth-century England, they were never used "upstairs."

Eggcups
Now that the reputation of eggs has been rehabilitated, their purchase may be warrented.

OTHER SPECIALIZED ITEMS

Many dinnerware patterns, especially informal ones, include such specialty items as covered soups, salt and pepper shakers, pitchers of varied sizes, covered butter dishes, bread trays, footed cake plates, strawberry bowls, cookie jars, canister sets, lazy Susans, ashtrays, coasters, and candlesticks. The names are, for the most part, self-explanatory.

It is not necessary to acquire every single item that is made in your pattern. Today, many people prefer to have these accessories in other materials, such as glass, stainless steel, or silver.

At a formal dinner, all the fine china need not match, but all the plates for each course should be the same. Silver or glass butter plates and glass salad or dessert plates may be used with any fine china.

CARE OF FINE CHINA

I would never put fine china in a dishwasher, although manufacturers today claim dinnerware is dishwasher-safe. If you do decide to wash dishes in a machine, there are certain guidelines to follow.

- Make sure the pieces are not touching or they'll rattle against each other when the machine is vibrating.
- Don't use a harsh detergent. (Most manufacturers specify which brands to use with their ware.)
- To avoid thumbprints and smears, let the ware cool before unloading the machine.
- Add two teaspoons of water softener to eliminate the build-up of film caused by hard water.

When washing fine china by hand, first rinse off excess food. To avoid scratches, cushion dinnerware in a towel-lined sink or use a plastic tub. Never use an abrasive to remove anything that's been baked on; you'll harm the glaze. Instead, soak it in hot (not boiling) water and, if necessary, use a plastic scouring pad. Don't use a rubber mat if the ware has a decoration of platinum, silver, or gold because a chemical reaction can occur between the precious metals and the rubber that will leave a brown mark on the plates. Dry with a soft, lint-free cloth.

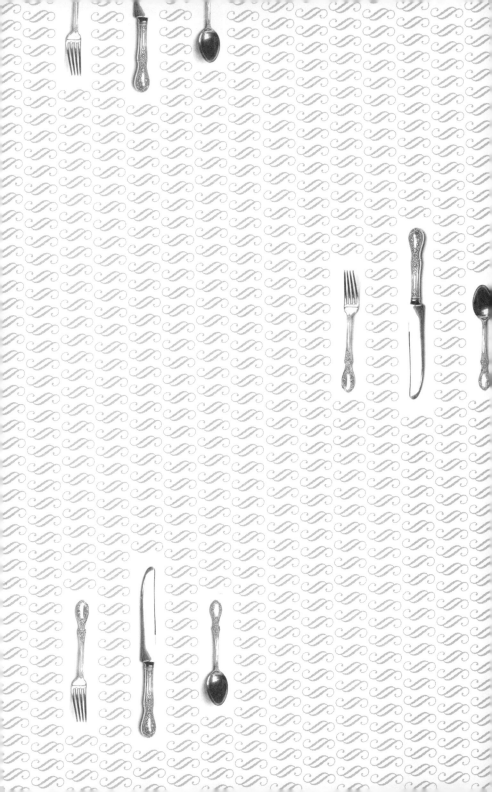

CHAPTER FIVE

GOBLETS, FLUTES, AND TUMBLERS

The highlight of my father's career was the visit of his majesty King Edward VII to Bishop's Hall in 1905. My father recalls that when he had to ask the king what he desired to drink, the answer, delivered in a Teutonic accent, was "visky and vater." I often think of this whenever I see King Edward VII depicted as speaking English with no accent at all.

Of course, the vessels used in the king's service were fine lead crystal. Once, fine glassware was extremely rare and priceless. During the Middle Ages, the method of producing it was known only to a few, and the glassmakers of Murano, Italy, were elevated to the level of nobility. By the early twentieth century, however, lead crystal was an easily acquired luxury.

Most people call fine glassware, crystal. But the word "crystal" simply means clear, uncolored glassware. When people refer to crystal, they mean lead crystal. A glass must be made of at least twenty-four percent lead to carry this appellation legally. Lead gives glass more weight, increases its resilience, and adds a brilliancy and sparkle. It is most often used to make glasses with cut patterns because it provides a thicker wall with which the cutter can work. It will also reflect a virtual rainbow of lights when polished.

In English estates, the glassware used for formal dining was all cut lead crystal. And what was used then is still very appropriate today.

There are glasses for sherry, white wine, red wine, and champagne, as well as glasses for brandy, port, and liqueurs. The major difference is in size; glasses have gotten much bigger. Another difference is that water was served in tumblers (unstemmed glasses), not goblets.

Today, fine table glasses are sold individually, not as place settings. Here are the pieces available in most stemware designs:

WINEGLASSES AND MORE

GOBLET

The largest piece of stemware, it holds from nine to twelve fluid ounces (266 to 355 milliliters). It is always used for water in formal dining, but at an informal meal its use is optional.

RED WINE

Today, with the exception of Waterford, most formal patterns offer just one size of red wineglass. In my day, there were separate glasses for claret (Bordeaux) and burgundy. Specially shaped wineglasses are widely available, but not in formal patterns (see below). An all-purpose wineglass will have a rounded bowl that tapers slightly toward the rim to contain the wine's bouquet.

WHITE WINE

A white wineglass has a bowl that is smaller than that of the red, and sides that are a little straighter, because white wine does not have as intense an aroma as red. It holds about six ounces (about 177 milliliters), but is never more than half-filled, in order to concentrate the wine's more delicate bouquet.

HOCK WINE

These are white wines from the Rhine Valley (and are named for their growing area, Hockenheim). Initially, Hock wines were served in a glass with a colored bowl to hide the wine's cloudiness, but today these wines are no longer cloudy. Queen Victoria, whose ancestors on her mother's side were from the house of Saxony Coberg, introduced Hock wines to England. Rhine wines are served in long-stemmed glasses with small, squared-off bowls. These, too, are often not available as part of a regular stemware pattern.

CHAMPAGNE

The most common shape available today is the flute, which has a long narrow bowl to preserve the effervescence of the bubbles. It has supplanted the traditional saucer champagne, which has a shallow, wide bowl, letting bubbles escape too quickly for today's tastes. In fact, a gentleman always used to carry his own swizzle stick, which he used to take out the bubbles, not make more.

WINE WARE

Because of the growing interest in fine wine, many manufacturers now produce glasses designed to bring out the optimum flavor of specific varietals. These include glasses for Bordeaux (white and red), chardonnay, Riesling, sauterne, Montrachet, pinot noir, sauvignon blanc, Beaujolais, burgundy, Chianti, zinfandel, rosé, and on and on. Wine connoisseurs may want these glasses. And because they are simple, unadorned clear glass they will be at home with any other formal stemware and can be used at formal dinners. If you are serving two different kinds of white wines—e.g. a chardonnay and a Riesling— or two different red wines, you must have separate glasses for each.

And remember, no new wine should ever be served in a previously used glass!

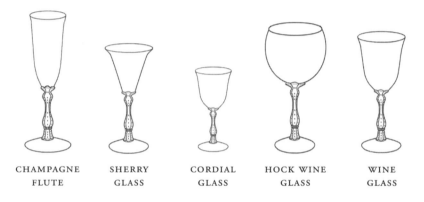

CHAMPAGNE   SHERRY   CORDIAL   HOCK WINE   WINE
  FLUTE   GLASS   GLASS   GLASS   GLASS

COCKTAIL

Strictly speaking, a cocktail glass shouldn't be included in a formal stemware grouping; cocktails are never served at the formal dinner table. But this glass is traditionally available in most stemware patterns, as is the cordial. A cocktail glass is shorter than a wineglass, with a smaller capacity, and it has a wider mouth. Most think of a martini glass when describing the prototypical shape.

CORDIAL

There are many different after-dinner drinks, and almost every one has its own special glass. As with wines, the general one in most stemware patterns is suitable for just about every type of liqueur. Cordial glasses are never flared, because the drink's aroma must be contained in the glass so that the drinker can savor it. These glasses have very small bowls because liqueurs are very concentrated and only a small amount is taken.

SHERRY

The one aperitif that is still used at a formal table, as it was when I was a butler; this glass is at the table to accompany the soup course. Today, it is rarely available in stemware patterns but is sold as a specialty glass. These are available in two different shapes, both on stems. One has a flared bowl; the other has a fuller base and tapered lip.

FOOTED ICED TEAS

A tall glass with a short stem, it is generously sized to accommodate ice cubes. Because iced tea is so frequently served in the southern United States, this glass is usually available there with most patterns.

BAR WARE

Whereas stemware is designed to be used at the dinner table, bar ware is used for beverages served before or after a formal dinner. But today, many stemware patterns do include a full range of bar ware. The most common types include:

TUMBLER OR HIGHBALL

These can be footed, straight-sided, flared, or rounded. Their capacity ranges from ten to fourteen ounces (296 to 414 milliliters). They are used for "tall" drinks such as rum and coke, or soda, milk, or fruitades.

OLD FASHIONED

Named after the drink, it's used for on-the-rocks beverages; in fact, it is often called an on-the-rocks glass. It has a capacity of about seven or eight ounces (207 to 237 milliliters). It is also available in a larger size, a double old-fashioned glass, with an eleven-ounce (325 milliliters) capacity.

WHISKEY AND SODA

This is the smaller edition of the highball with a capacity of about eight ounces (237 milliliters). It's much more widely used in Europe, because Europeans are less likely to use ice in their drinks and therefore don't need glasses with such a large capacity.

ICED TEA

A larger version of the highball with a capacity of around twenty ounces (592 milliliters), these are ideal for summertime drinks that require lots of ice cubes.

SPECIALTY GLASSES

PILSNER

Named for a famous German beer, this is a tall glass on a short low stem with a narrow base that tapers up gracefully to an elegant height.

BEER GOBLET

A deeper and more capacious version of the water goblet.

BEER MUG

The advantage of a mug is that its handle keeps you from warming up the beverage with your hands. (A beer stein, the traditional German vessel for beer, is a mug with a lid and is usually ceramic.) In my day, some mugs had round bases so that the beer had to be consumed completely before they could be put down.

WHISKEY SOUR

A long, narrow glass on a very short stem, it's specifically designed for this mixture of lemon, sugar, and whiskey.

PARFAIT

This was not originally designed for serving ice cream but for a cordial in which a series of heavy liqueurs are poured one on another, rainbow style, until the glass is full.

BRANDY/BENEDICTINE

These are taller than most generic cordial glasses and have a tulip-like shape.

COGNAC

Slightly taller than the average cordial glass, it holds about an ounce more than a brandy/benedictine.

BRANDY SNIFTERS

These are designed to enable the drinker to warm the brandy in his hands and thus be able to enjoy and savor the brandy's aroma. This glass is always on a low stem with a very wide bowl that tapers up to a narrow opening. They come in various sizes, from five to twenty-five ounces (148 to 739 milliliters). A glass should never be more than one-third full.

SPARKLING GLASSWARE

One of the cardinal rules of table setting is to make sure the glassware sparkles. Here are my special tips:

- After the glasses have been placed on the table, a nice finishing touch is to use two old silk handkerchiefs to add a final shine on them. Then they'll have no fingerprints and will sparkle with candlelight.
- I was taught how to dry an expensive, thin, wineglass by holding the bowl in a cloth in my left hand and gently drying it with the other end of the cloth in my right hand. Never hold on to the foot of the stem and then try to dry the bowl, because some of these glasses are very fragile and one can easily snap off the stem. This is what the footmen called "screwing off the stem."

One little trick I was shown by the footman when I was growing up (of which my father wouldn't have approved) was to make music with the large ornamental glass bowls. These had broad, flat rims, and we would wet a finger and rub it around the circumference of one rim. This would eventually cause a reverberation that was amplified by the large bowl, resulting in a deep, booming sound that could be kept going for a long time. Perhaps this is not the most constructive advice to pass on, but I hope that the rest of what has been written in this chapter will open your eyes to crystal's great beauty.

WASHING GLASSWARE TODAY

While most manufacturers claim that crystal can go into the dishwasher, you'll be happier with the results if you wash fine stemware by hand. Hard water or chemicals used to treat water can react with the chemicals in the washing detergent, creating a film on the glass that is difficult to remove. (If a film does develop, try adding white vinegar to the rinse water.)

Wash glasses before the rest of the dishes. Place each glass in the sink separately and wash it with warm, soapy water. Use water of a temperature that is comfortable for you, because then there is less of a chance of dropping the glass. Scalding water is not really necessary and the extreme change in temperature may cause the glass to crack.

Glasses should be rinsed in water that is the same temperature as the water that is used for washing. Because glass is sensitive to changes in temperature, don't put a cold glass in hot water. If the water is exceptionally hard, use a water softener. Hard water has a high concentration of minerals, notably calcium and magnesium carbonate. In terms of health, it's harmless. But it won't lather well, and it causes spots and filmy surfaces on glasses and scaly lime deposits on your pipes.

To avoid scratching the crystal, take your rings off before washing. If the glass has a flared rim, handle it a little more carefully, i.e., carry only one piece at a time in each hand. (If the rims are straight-sided or curve inward, you can dispense with this advice.) Use a rubber nozzle to prevent glass from hitting the spout. Dry with a soft, lint-free towel. Linen cloths are best. (Many people recommend cloth diapers for the job.) Check for water spots before putting the glass away, and wipe any off immediately because they can leave permanent marks.

⤞ HOW TABLEWARE ⤝
ONCE WAS WASHED

In the great houses, they used oval wooden bowls banded with galvanized iron hoops to hold the wood staves in position, as well as lead-lined sinks and draining boards. The lead-lined sinks were used to cover the wooden sinks to make them waterproof. The idea was to prevent any damage to silver, china, or glass, as a slight knock against either wood or lead wasn't likely to chip or break china or glass or scratch beautifully polished silver.

To prepare his mixture for washing up, the odd man (Americans might call him a handyman). would use a handful of washing soda (to soften the water), then, with a galvanized wire whisk, beat up a lovely soapy lather using soft green soap.

Natural sponges were used to wash the silver and glass. When these sponges were first bought, they contained an appreciable amount of sand and tiny shells, which, if not removed, might scratch the highly polished surface of the silver. To de-sand them, one would soak them in cold water for a day or two, continually rinsing them and changing the water until all traces of sand were washed out. Then they were felt all over to see if any tiny shells were still in the sponge fiber. Only then was the sponge put to use. Eventually the sponge became full of soap that wouldn't rinse out so it would have to be soaked in lukewarm water, to which would be added ammonia. This would eventually rid the sponge of the accumulated soap.

Each piece of silver, china, or glass had to be washed and handled separately, and after being washed in soapy water would be rinsed in very hot water and dried with clean linen cloths known as "pantry rubbers."

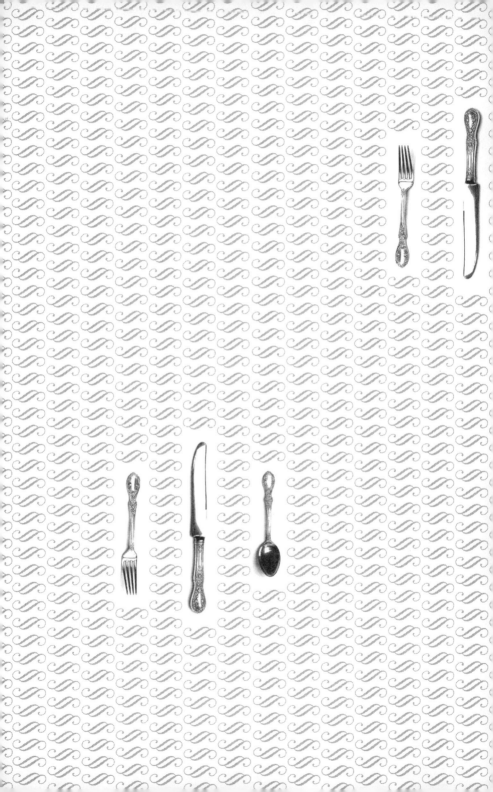

CHAPTER SIX

THE COMPLETE TABLE

Making a table look good involves a lot more than just selecting the perfect china, glass, and silver. Just as with the little black dress, the accessories make the difference.

TABLE ATTIRE

Just as important to the art of the table as beautiful and well-kept china, glass, and silver, are table linens. In my time, beautiful linen damask tablecloths were the norm. (Damask can be woven in virtually every kind of cloth on jacquard looms that allow for complex repeat patterns.)

But, after World War II, with the scarcity of household help, place mats came into vogue, because they required much less care. The development of synthetic fabrics in the '50s and '60s brought easy-care blends to the market, simplifying laundering as well as making tablecloths more affordable. Today, either place mats or tablecloths are acceptable at the formal table, but tablecloths do unify the setting visually as well as helping to lower the noise level in the room. They also add a note of drama and glamour.

Traditionally, only white cloths or mats and napkins were used, but, as previously noted, colors have entered the picture. Remember that if you decide to use any color at all, it should match or contrast well with the dinnerware pattern.

TABLECLOTHS

The size of the tablecloth is critical. To calculate it, measure the length and width of the dining table and allow for an overhang—the distance between the edge of the table and the hem. There is no hard-and-fast rule about overhang, but in general, the longer the table, the deeper it should be. At a formal setting it should range from twelve to eighteen inches (thirty-one to forty-six centimeters). If your tables are round, the drop should hang to the floor.

Also, when using a tablecloth, the middle crease must be placed in an absolutely straight and unwavering line down the exact center of the table.

When the staffs of the great houses set a table, they usually covered the bare table first with a baize cloth—a thick, coarse, woolen fabric that resembles felt. It is the material used on pool tables. Today, you can either use this or make your own padding from an old blanket or piece of foam-backed vinyl that's been cut to fit the table. Custom table pads made of layered insulation and topped with flannel are widely available.

PLACE MATS

There really was a person named Doyley who lived in London during the seventeenth century. He was a London tailor who was arguably the first to put a small linen mat under a bowl (to keep the bowl from moving around). The modern place mat evolved from this concept and today comes in assorted shapes and sizes in a variety of materials: wood, bamboo, glass, mirrored tile, and stainless steel, as well as all manner of textiles. The most popular sizes are twelve by eighteen inches (thirty-one by forty-six centimeters) and fourteen by twenty inches (thirty-six by fifty-one centimeters), and they accommodate an entire setting.

I understand that table runners have also gained in popularity, although I've never personally seen them used. In any case, they are not appropriate for formal dinners. They are dressier than place mats and easier to handle than a tablecloth. A runner is approximately fourteen to seventeen inches (thirty-six to forty-three centimeters) wide; its drop should be about fifteen inches (thirty-eight centimeters).

If the formal dinner table to be used has a particularly beautiful surface, the table can be bare of all napery except napkins.

NAPKINS

Most napkins are square. For a formal, multicourse meal, they should range from twenty-two to twenty-six inches (fifty-six to sixty-six centimeters) square. Paper napkins are never used. At a formal meal, the napkin should match the tablecloth. (At informal ones, contrasting color can provide a stylish accent.)

There are numerous ways to fold napkins, but if a napkin is monogrammed, then it must be folded so that the monogram shows. Traditionally, the staff would fold the snowy white damask napkins into a special shape, of which there were many, such as a single miter, double miter, rose, fan, slipper, lazy waiter, pig's face, and a host of others. I usually chose the single miter, which as its name implies, looks rather like a bishop's miter and was a tall, imposing–looking fold, especially when there were twenty or thirty around a table. Today, it is acceptable (indeed many find it preferable) that the napkin be simply folded and placed on the service plate. Formal-sized napkins are folded three times in each direction to make a smaller square. The two sides are then folded under, making a loosely rolled rectangle.

Putting napkins at the side of an empty plate at a formal setting is incorrect. They are placed in the center of the place mat (or, today, the service plate). The napkins go on the left side only when a first course is put on the table before guests are seated at less formal occasions. When the napkin is placed on the side, it is never put under the forks but to the left of them. If the napkins are monogrammed, the monogram should face the diner.

Napkin rings are never used at formal dinners. Their original purpose before the days of washing machines was to enable the napkin to be identified by the user and put into service more than once. At the great houses, a clean napkin would be used for every meal, so no napkin rings were ever needed. Today, napkin rings are employed as decorative accessories.

LAUNDRY

CARING FOR TABLE LINENS, THEN

The laundry was an integral part of most estates, including at Nidd Hall, where my father was a butler from 1923 to 1934. There were three laundry maids. They resided in a cottage directly opposite the laundry and lived a separate life, quite apart from the main indoor staff, buying and cooking all of their own meals.

The laundry itself consisted of two huge rooms. The first was the washing room, where all the appliances were run by DC electricity (made on the estate) and the machinery was driven by many wheels and pulleys powered by large flapping belts. There were two huge boilers for the clothes, which were heated by a coke boiler. There was a line of sinks below a huge window and slatted boards to stand on. A spin dryer powered by the belts and pulleys effectively squeezed out the excess water from the wash. There was a grass-covered drying green about two hundred yards (approximately one-hundred-and-eighty-three meters) from the laundry, and the wet clothes were put into a large wicker basket and pushed on a trolley to the many lines on the green, where everything was dried in the sunshine and fresh air.

The other large room was for airing, mangling, and ironing. There were airing racks that ran between the drying cupboard and the vats. Then there was the ubiquitous mangle at the far end (a mangle is a machine that presses sheets between two rollers). At the other end and also in front of the large window was the ironing shelf extending the full width of the room, where the three laundry maids did the ironing at three stations. One of the three round, ledged, and coke-filled stoves was always ready to heat the many flat irons that were used.

When all the washing and ironing was completed, it was all packed into square, lidded, wicker linen baskets, and the odd man would take it on a trolley from the laundry into the hall along a long white-tiled passage. Then he'd send it upstairs on the lift to the housemaid linen room, where the housemaids would sort it into the slatted shelves.

Taking Care of Table Linens Today

While everyone would no doubt appreciate having three laundry maids on staff at their home, this obviously isn't reality anymore. But since good-quality table linens do require care and attention, try the following tips.

Keep all your linens—bedding and towels as well as table linen—separate from clothing, not on open shelving but in a closed, well-ventilated closet. Starch linens every few weeks. A thin layer of starch will protect fabric from dirt. Don't iron linens when the iron is too hot or you may scorch them. Make sure the sole plate of the iron is clean before you use it. Wipe it with a mixture of equal amounts of vinegar and water to remove mineral deposits.

For storing good tablecloths, use tissue paper, not plastic bags, because bags trap moisture and mildew may set in. Since seldom-used linens wrinkle when stored, it is easier to put them away laundered but not ironed. Don't store soiled linens; stains do set and are much harder to remove the longer they've been there.

OTHER TABLE ACCESSORIES

PLACE CARDS AND MENUS

Place cards are a wonderful help for both the hostess and her guests. They direct everyone to his or her seat, eliminating the confusion that occurs when guests enter the dining room and hover behind chairs, wondering where to sit. Place cards should be about two-and-a-half inches long and stand three-quarters-of-an-inch high (approximately eleven-and-a-half by sixteen-and-a-half centimeters is a standard size in the U.K.) when folded. They are usually plain, or they can be bordered in gold or silver. The guest's name should be legibly written, with writing that is large enough to be easily seen. Place cards may be put on top of and in the center of the napkin if the napkin is placed on the place mat or service plate, but if unsteady there, they can be put on the tablecloth above the place mat or service plate at the exact center of the serving. Thoughtful hostesses will write the guest's name on both sides of the place card, so that persons sitting across the table will know who they are.

Menu Cards

Menu cards are really a courtesy to your guests. They allow people to pace themselves though the meal. If you're serving six or seven courses, guests might want to skip one or two!

You can either order menu cards from a stationer or make your own by cutting them out of any white or cream paper stock. A good size is four-and-a-half inches by six-and-a-half inches (eleven by seventeen centimeters). If you have an engraved monogram die from your stationery, you can have it stamped on the menu as well as on matching place cards.

Place the menu between two settings or in a special holder at the top center of the place setting. Menus can be written, printed or typed, but the handwriting should be identical on the place and menu cards. If your party is to celebrate a special occasion, indicate that on the top of the menu card and include the date. A place card can simply be folded tent-like and doesn't need a holder, but inexpensive holders for both menus and place cards are widely available, both online and at restaurant supply outlets. Fine silver ones can also be readily found.

SERVING PIECES

These are all the dishes, platters and bowls from which food is served, and of course, no formal dinner—or even an informal one—is possible without them.

Serve ware is available in sterling silver, silver plate, and stainless steel, as well as other metals such as brass, bronze, and copper, and all types of ceramics. It doesn't matter which material you select.

PLATTERS

These oval serving dishes range in size from ten inches to twenty-four inches.

Chop Plate

We didn't use these, but a chop plate is a round platter, originally created for serving chops (as its name implies). It is also useful for hors d'oeuvres before dinner.

Serving Bowls

These are available in a round shape (called a "nappy" in trade parlance) or oval (dubbed "baker" by china makers).

GRAVY BOAT
WITH UNDERPLATE

COVERED VEGETABLE
BOWL

Divided Vegetable Dish

A multicompartment serving dish that is not always available in all patterns. It is usually only used for very small dinners.

Covered Vegetable

The cover lets you keep food warm for a longer period of time. If the ware is ovenproof, it's usually called a casserole.

Gravy or Sauce Boat

These are available either attached to a stand or with a separate saucer. (The saucer can do double duty as a pickle or olive plate.)

Sugar Bowl

Sugar bowls come with or without lids. They are made in a standard size or in a smaller after-dinner size to match an after-dinner service. They are put on the table and filled with caster sugar (see glossary) and a serving spoon.

CREAMER   SUGAR BOWL   TEAPOT   COFFEE POT
WITH LID

Creamer

It is primarily meant as a container for cream and milk but can also be drafted for serving gravies and syrups. Creamers are also available in an after-dinner coffee size.

Coffeepot/Teapot

These come in many sizes. There are individual ones for breakfast (or a large one to be kept on the sideboard), after-dinner-size servers and eight to twelve cup (two to three liters) containers. A teapot is shorter and squatter than a coffeepot.

Pitcher
These come in a wide variety of sizes, for everything from syrup and honey to water and iced tea.

TABLE DECORATION

CENTERPIECES

There is no rule that decrees that the center decoration has to be silver candelabra flanked with bowls of flowers. In modern times, the choices are almost infinite—from beautifully arranged containers of fresh fruits such as lemons and limes, to floral arrangements that can range from sprays of lilac and lavender, to a formal mixed arrangement. Plastic artificial flowers are a bad choice, but silk, glass, or porcelain ones are appropriate. It's really whatever you prefer. I have seen a silver rugby ball used or even a large decorative salt cellar, but I like the old-fashioned ideas best.

Whatever you select, make sure that the size of the centerpiece is in proportion to the size of the table, and low enough for guests to speak across the table without having to peer through a table arrangement.

OTHER DECORATIONS

As for candles, they should be brand new. They are lit before the guests come to the table and not extinguished until the guests leave the dining room. If the candles supply the only light for the table, there should be a candle for each person. You'll need two to four candelabra (branched candleholders), depending on the length of the table and the number of guests. Make sure that the flame is not at the eye level of the diners. The lighting in a normal dining room is a center chandelier and wall sconces with imitation candles—all electric lights.

Dishes or compotes filled with candied fruit, thin chocolate mints, or other candies may be put on the table wherever there are equally spaced, empty spots. They stay there for the entire meal and can be passed after the dessert course. Nuts with nutcrackers can also be put on the table, either in large silver dishes or in small individual ones at each place. They are served with the fruit course.

Nowadays going around to the stately homes that are open to the public, one often sees the dining room table laid up as though for dinner, but this display pales in comparison to the real thing when the scene was animated by gorgeously dressed ladies and gents who were waited on by immaculately dressed menservants all trained to do their jobs, serving good food and wine. This was really the peak of gracious living.

Back then, when the table was ready just before eight p.m., the butler would go into the dining room, and his eagle eye would inspect the table from all angles. Woe betide the under butler should a cruet or wine glass be out of line or a napkin not folded in precisely the same way as the others and all lined up along the table like guardsmen! The same went for the chairs, which stood precisely at each place, ready to be eased under the guests when they sat down. Then, when the first course was on the hot plate outside the dining room door and we had all taken our positions behind the chairs, the butler would sound the great Chinese gong and announce to her grace that, "Dinner is served."

PART III

AT THE PARTY

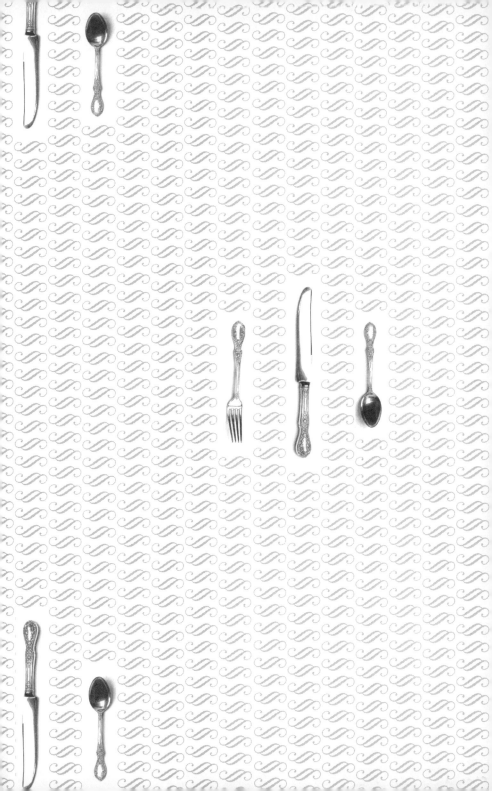

CHAPTER SEVEN

HOW TO BE THE PERFECT HOSTESS
AND THE PERFECT GUEST

THE HOST OR HOSTESS

The key ingredients for a successful party are simple: interesting guests, stimulating conversation, good food, and good service. But the most important element of all is a warm and welcoming atmosphere. The host and hostess's main task is to make guests feel relaxed and comfortable. The rules of etiquette are there to help you do just that. They are based on common sense and are designed to make things flow more easily. Don't be overwhelmed by them. Sometimes rules can be bent, or even broken. There are often occasions that, while formal in nature, do not require strict adherence to protocol. For events such as these, do only what is easy for you to handle, and eliminate details that would be difficult or seem unnatural. Pick and choose the elements that are suitable for the way you live, and use the following information as a guide.

Planning

Once you've decided to give a formal party, your first step is to choose the date and time and then hire staff and/or caterers. (If you are hiring a caterer, make sure that he or she is available on the day you've chosen before sending out invitations.)

In these contemporary times, even the very wealthy seldom have large enough staffs to serve a true formal dinner, so hiring help is necessary. The best way to go about finding help is to ask a friend who has recently hosted a party. If you are at someone else's catered event and you like the service, ask the waiter for the caterer's business card. Keep names and numbers of waiters you've seen at friends' homes. Call a local college's job-placement office for referrals to students who have had experience waiting or bartending. Call bartending and cooking schools, as well.

To create a gracious and calm atmosphere, the general rule calls for a trained waiter to serve every six guests. And of course, you'll need someone else—caterers or a cook—who can produce a festive multi-course meal, because it is this procession of courses that invokes the spirit of welcome, plenty, and celebration. Select a caterer at least a month in advance. Again, get recommendations from friends. Ask two or three caterers for estimates, and be sure to check references before selecting one.

INVITATIONS

For a true formal dinner, formal invitations, either handwritten or engraved, are in order, and they must be in the third person. While it may seem obvious, be sure that the invitation includes the date, time, and place.

Invitations should be sent three to six weeks before the event, depending on your community's own customs. If you don't hear from someone to whom you have sent an invitation, don't hesitate to call; the person is either being thoughtless and needs a gentle reminder, or the invitation may have been lost in the mail.

Guest List

When deciding whom to invite, make sure you have a compatible collection of people, but not too compatible. Don't invite too many friends with too much in common. That's one sure way to guarantee a boring evening. You need an interesting mix to spark conversation. Blend office friends with relatives, neighbors with friends. And remember that having an equal number of men and women is not essential. There is nothing wrong with having two women sit side by side.

The Seating Plan

The easiest way to organize your table is to draw a diagram on a large piece of cardboard. Write the name of each guest on an individual slip of paper or a Post-it note. Then, move names around until you come up with the optimum solution. Be sure that couples are not seated next to each other; you want guests to mingle. If you are giving the party in someone's honor, the seats to the right of the host and hostess are the places of honor.

The Staff or Additional Help

Any large party will require outside helpers, and seeing that they are well-trained is crucial to the staging of a successful dinner. But even if you have hired trained professionals, it is up to you, the host or hostess, to let them know exactly how you want things to be done. And it is you who ultimately must make sure that the table is set properly, the flowers are beautifully arranged, and the bar is well-stocked (including plenty of ice).

At formal dinners today, the role of the butler is still the central one, just as it was in my day. Indeed, the butler orchestrates the entire service. Well before the day of the party, the hostess should review all the details of the evening with him, including how the waiters are to be attired. On the evening of the event, shortly before the guests arrive, the hostess should check the dining room and give any last-minute instructions to the butler, including confirming with him the time he is to announce dinner. The butler will then go over last-minute details with the staff and make his tour of the waiters, inspecting their apparel, including shoes, hair, and fingernails, as I did and still do.

THE GUESTS

ETIQUETTE

To the uninitiated, formal dining etiquette may seem like a foreign language. But it's really a logical system that's arisen from both practicality and tradition. Manners are just tools to help us get along in a complicated world. They're one of the ways we show consideration for others and they're meant to help us, not to intimidate us. Once you understand their rationale, you'll never have to think about minding your manners again.

FASHIONABLY ON TIME

The exact time you should arrive at a formal dinner party varies with the custom of your particular community. If you had been invited to a formal event in pre-World War II England, you would have been expected to be there a half hour before dinner. In the great houses of Great Britain, dinner was served at the stroke of eight. Today, a general rule of thumb to follow is not to arrive more than twenty minutes after the time stated on the invitation.

At a formal dinner party, guests were not and are not now expected to bring gifts. In my days of private service, the only exception to this rule would be if it were a birthday party for the host or hostess. If it were for the host, guests might bring a special bottle of vintage port, champagne, claret, or burgundy; and if it were for the hostess's birthday, a small item of jewelry or a special perfume might be appropriate.

Party Logistics

When you enter the living room, find your hostess to say hello. If you are offered a drink before you find her, you should refuse it. Good manners require you to speak to your hosts first before accepting their hospitality. After you have a drink, if you want a refill it is perfectly all right to ask the butler for another one.

When *hors d'oeuvres* are passed, take just one, not three or four. It is the waiter's job to see that they are passed so that you don't have to ask for a second one. At a formal dinner party, it's not usual to have a great deal of food served during cocktails. It's hardly necessary when a five-or six-course meal is in the offing. During cocktail service in the old days there was not a great deal of food, only nibbles such as little biscuits or almonds.

Quick Tips

One of your main responsibilities as a guest is to socialize and help get the party going. During cocktail hour, make an effort to meet people you don't already know. Husbands and wives should mingle, not huddle together, excluding others. When dinner is announced, try not to linger in the living room. The food is obviously ready, and slow-moving guests cause problems for the kitchen.

At a formal dinner, do not bring your unfinished drink to the table. Leave it in the living room. Women may either leave their evening bags in the living room or bring them into the dining room. If a bag is small enough, it can sit on one's lap. Otherwise, place it well underneath the chair so the waiter doesn't trip over it. It's acceptable for guests to make their way to the dining room at random with one exception: If you are the female guest of honor, you are escorted by the host. If you are the male guest of honor, the hostess will escort you.

TABLE TALK

Once you are seated, you should begin conversation with your dinner partner. It's rude to ignore him or her to scan the table to see who else is there. And remember to talk with both of your partners—the people on your right and left. Introduce yourself if you didn't meet during cocktails. Don't wait for someone else to initiate the conversation. Try to draw both dinner partners out, and show an interest in what they have to say.

Remember that the essence of good conversation is to be more interested in hearing the other person's point of view than expressing your own. Try to find something to talk about that will interest both of you. If you feel that you have nothing in common, you must still make an effort and not let your discomfort show. To avoid these awkward moments, most hostesses favor round tables, because it's easier for three or four people to join in a single conversation.

SITTING PRETTY

Do sit straight but not stiffly, leaning slightly against the back of the chair. Slouching and slumping are not acceptable. And don't tilt your chair back. Besides the fact that it's dangerous, it's also very hard on the chair's legs. Throwing your arm over the back of your chair or that of your dinner partner is also frowned upon.

The best thing to do with your hands when you are not eating is to keep them in your lap. Following this rule will automatically keep you from fidgeting with your flatware or playing with bread crumbs. It is perfectly acceptable to rest your hands and wrists on the table, but not your entire forearm. Although we've all heard the "never put your elbows on the table" rule, in some instances, it's all right. For example, in order to hear someone across from you, you may have to lean forward. But elbows should never rest on the table while you are eating.

NAPKIN ETIQUETTE

At normal dinners, you usually put your napkin on your lap as soon as you are seated. At a formal dinner, you wait for your hostess to put hers on her lap first. And do place the napkin on your lap, not under your chin or tucked into your shirt. If the napkin is large, open it just halfway, without giving it a violent shake.

Never use your napkin as a handkerchief or as a washcloth; pat—don't rub—your mouth. If you need to leave the table during a meal, put the napkin either on the left side of your plate (soiled part turned underneath, out of sight) or on your chair. When the meal is finished, put the napkin on the left side of your plate, or, if the plates have been removed, put it in the center of the setting. It should not be refolded or crumpled up. Lay it on the table in loose folds. At a dinner party, the hostess lays her napkin on the table as a signal that the meal is over. Guests then place theirs on the table. Never before.

When To Begin Eating

If the table is a large one, it is not necessary to wait until everyone has been served. The hostess may say, as soon as the first two or three guests have been given their food, "Please start. Your dinner will get cold if you wait." If she says nothing, it's all right to pick up your knife and fork after three or four people have been served. If you are at a small, round table with six to eight people, however, wait until all the guests at your table have been served.

How To Be Served

When the waiter presents you with the serving platter on your left side, pick up both the spoon and fork to serve yourself. Take the serving fork in your left hand and the spoon in your right hand. After you have helped yourself, put the serving spoon and fork side by side back on the plate. If there are several foods on the tray, take the meat first, then the vegetables. Take a moderate helping of each.

Place vegetables on your plate, not on any side dish, which in all probability is the bread-and-butter plate. If the course presented includes another layer of food underneath—toast or lettuce, for example—-don't pick off the top but take the entire portion. As a courtesy to the last person served, make sure to leave enough food on the platter so he or she has a choice from several portions. Always take the portion nearest you. After being served, thank the server.

Which Knife and Fork To Use

The universally recognized way to set a table is to place the flatware on the table in the order of its use, starting from the outside in. But there are still some iconoclasts who insist on setting out flatware by size, leaving you to puzzle out the correct utensil for each course. If you make a mistake, don't put the silver back on the table; just quietly go ahead and use it. And don't offend the hostess by rearranging an improperly set table.

There are two methods for cutting food on your plate: European and American. In the European, or continental, style, the knife is held in the right hand and the fork in the left. The tines of the fork face down when the food is cut and the fork, still in the left hand, is brought to the mouth, tines down. In the American method, the fork starts in the left hand, the knife in the right, but after the food has been cut, the knife is placed flat on the plate and the fork is switched to the free right hand and turned right side up. It is then brought to the mouth in the right hand. The knife may also be used as a pusher, if necessary. Both styles are correct.

Eating Bread and Butter

When you sit down, you'll find the butter spreader placed across the butter plate. Do not cut bread with it: Always break bread with your fingers. The spreader is only used for buttering. Do not butter an entire roll or slice of bread at once. Tear off a small piece and butter this only.

Table Rules

Try to take a little bit of everything that is offered, even if it is a food you don't like. Then, quietly leave it on your plate without making an issue of it. If you are allergic to something, you don't need to say anything to your hostess unless it's very obvious to her that you are not eating. In that case, wait until after dinner.

When a relish or condiment tray is passed, put your selections on the butter plate, or if there isn't one, put it on the plate that is in front of you. Never take a single olive, strip of carrot, or celery directly from the condiment tray and put it in your mouth. Always place it on the plate first. Then pass the tray to the person next to you.

When presented with a gravy boat, ladle a modest amount—don't drown your meat. Replace the ladle to the side of the sauceboat; otherwise the ladle will get gravy on the back of it, which is messy for the next guest. You may sop up gravy with bread by putting a small piece down on the gravy and then eating it with your fork, not your fingers.

Sometimes, lemons are wrapped in cheesecloth to prevent seeds and squirts from escaping. If they are not, insert the tines of your fork into the lemon wedge and squeeze it over the food, using your other hand as a shield.

There are no rules about eating the fresh parsley sprigs or lemon rinds that are served as garnishes. If you don't want them, just move the garnishes to the side of your plate.

If you have bitten into something inedible, like a piece of gristle, don't spit it into your napkin. Put your fork up to your mouth and remove it; put it on your plate where you can bury it under some food so it is not visible.

If you are missing a piece of flatware or if you have dropped one, catch the eye of the waiter and tell him what you need.

Never put flatware down on the table after you've begun to eat. When resting between bites, place the knife and fork across each other; this signals the waiter that you have not finished. If you have finished, put the knife and fork parallel to each other in the middle of the plate; otherwise the server will not know whether you have finished eating or not.

Don't insult the cook by seasoning your food before you taste it. To serve yourself from an individual salt dish if there is no spoon, use the tip of your clean knife blade to take a little, or else take a pinch with your thumb and forefinger. But to be correct, there must always be a salt spoon in a salt cellar.

Savor the meal and eat slowly. It encourages conversation and conviviality.

Do not blow on hot foods or beverages. If you have burned your mouth, take a quick sip of water to lessen the burn's effect.

When you are served a hot beverage, to test its temperature, take a single sip from the side of the spoon. If it's too hot, give the beverage time to cool before you start to drink it.

Once you've put a bite of food on your fork or spoon, you must consume it in its entirety. It's impolite to half-eat or half-sip foods such as ice cream or soup.

Each time you take a mouthful, lean over your plate. If anything drops, it will fall on the plate, not on your lap or on the tablecloth. Never pile food high on your fork or spoon. Take only enough to chew and swallow in one easy bite.

Chew with your mouth closed, and try not to smack your lips. Don't speak with your mouth full. You might need to talk with a little in your mouth, because sometimes you can't wait until you have swallowed everything before you answer a question. But if you only take a little at a time, you will always be able to join the conversation.

If you should happen to spill something on the tablecloth, scoop it up with your knife and put it on the side of the plate. If you spill something on yourself, wrap your napkin around your finger, dip it in your water glass, and rub the spot. If something is spilled while you are being served, don't panic. It's up to the waiter to take care of it. If you've spilled wine, use your napkin to soak it up until the waiter arrives with towels to place between the tablecloth and the table. To take out the stain, he'll probably sprinkle the spot with salt or soda water or some other cleaning substance.

Try to eat quietly. The essence of good table manners is unobtrusiveness. Not only does noise impede conversation, the sounds of someone scraping his or her plate or chewing on ice are unpleasant to hear.

If you don't want wine, just gesture toward your wineglass and say, "No, thank you" to the waiter. Don't turn your wineglass upside down. Conversely, if you want more wine, wait until it is passed, which it will be periodically.

Do one thing at a time. If you want to sip your wine, rest your knife and fork on the plate.

If you break a wineglass, you should replace it. Do your best to find out from the hostess where the glass was bought.

Reach only for things that are close enough to grasp in one fluid motion. Otherwise, ask another guest to pass it to you.

Try to keep pace with the other diners so you don't delay the waiters in clearing the table for the next course.

When the waiters clear the table, don't assist them by handing them anything. You can help by leaning to one side if the chairs are so close together that clearing is difficult. Lay your knife and fork together in a straight line on the plate when you are finished. If they are crossed, it means you are still eating.

There should be no smoking at a dinner table during dinner. In my time, only the men smoked there, after the ladies had left the room. Even if there are ashtrays on the table, don't light up until the dessert course is finished.

Finger bowls are meant for fingers only, not your entire hand. Dip the tips of your fingers in the water one hand at a time, and dry them on your napkin.

Never apply lipstick at the table. For one thing, you then will avoid smearing lipstick on the rim of your glass and the napkin.

Don't get up from the table until your hostess does.

TOASTS

Sometimes, a formal meal is given in someone's honor, in which case toasts are an expected part of the evening. If the host or hostess does not make a toast first, you may do so after the main course. Rise to your feet, and if you have trouble getting everyone's attention, rap on a glass with an unused knife or fork (not too hard). Your toast may be a word of thanks for a splendid evening or an anecdote or story about the guest of honor. Whatever you say should be short and to the point. After finishing the toast, raise your glass to the person you are toasting and take a sip of wine.

If toasting is informal, guests stay seated while raising their glasses. For more commemorative occasions such as a wedding anniversary, all the guests rise, raise their glasses, and take a sip of wine. Nondrinking guests may raise their empty glasses or a glass of whatever else they may be drinking, except water, because some people believe that toasting with water is bad luck.

Large groups do not clink their glasses. There is a school of thought that holds that glasses should be clinked at an unequal height, never at the same level. If those raising a toast are seated too far apart for their glasses to touch, just raising the glass itself is sufficient. The person being toasted remains seated and doesn't raise his or her glass, but acknowledges the toast by a smile, a nod, and a thank you. The honoree then stands up and says a few words either directly after being toasted or a little later, perhaps at the end of the dessert course.

WHEN THE MEAL IS OVER

The hostess may ask the women guests to follow her into the living room for liqueurs and coffee (or these may be served at the dinner table). It is up to the host to tell the men guests whether they will have coffee at the table or move into the living room. But in my experience, it will take a lot of persuading to get the male guests out of the dining room before they have had their port, brandy, and cigars. While separating the sexes after dinner is a longstanding custom, today, many hostesses find it old-fashioned and prefer men to join the women in the living room.

When after-dinner coffee is served, it's all right to ask if it's decaffeinated. If it's not and you choose not to have any, just say no thank you, and leave it at that. Remember not to leave your spoon in your coffee cup, but put it on the side on the saucer.

Don't even think about going home until forty-five minutes after everyone has left the table. If you leave too early, you are sending a message to the hostess that you haven't had a good time. If there is a guest of honor, there is no reason you can't leave before he or she does (unless it is a high-ranking government official), provided you say good-bye. If you are the guest of honor, keep in mind that some people will feel they shouldn't go home until you do.

Also be aware that many guests will take your leaving as a lead and go home when you do. After saying good-bye to the host and hostess, it's important to leave right away. A guest who lingers can be exasperating for the host and hostess who want to get back to their other guests. It can also break up the party.

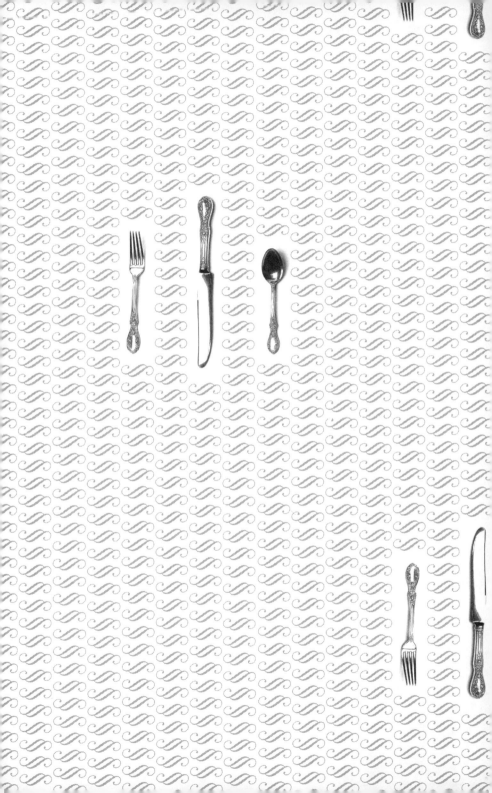

CHAPTER EIGHT

HOW TO EAT EVERYTHING FROM A(RTICHOKES) TO Z(ABAGLIONE)

One of the most essential aspects of good table manners is knowing how to eat all those troublesome foods one encounters when dining out. I hope that this chapter will provide a helpful guide to steer you away from social catastrophes.

COCKTAIL HOUR

CHERRY TOMATOES
These are eaten with your fingers during cocktails, but with a knife and fork when served in a salad or another course at the table. Try to select one that's small enough to put in your mouth whole, because they squirt. Close your lips tightly before chewing.

CHEESE
Cheese is spread or placed on a cracker with the knife that accompanies each cheese, and the cracker with cheese is eaten by hand.

COCKTAIL TRIMMINGS

It's perfectly acceptable to eat the olives, cherries, or onions that are in your drink. If they are served on a toothpick or cocktail pick, there's no problem. Just remove them from the drink and enjoy them. But if there is no pick, drink enough of the cocktail so that you don't wet your fingers, then lift the olive or cherry out, and eat it. (Avoid orange slices, because they are too messy—it's hard to chew the pulp off the rind gracefully.)

CRUDITÉS

When fresh vegetables and dips are offered, remember that you can only dip the vegetable into the sauce once, and never after you have taken a bite. I hope that this is obvious to you.

HOT HORS D'OEUVRES

Wait a few minutes until it cools down before you try to eat one. It can really burn the inside of your mouth if you pop one in while it is still steaming hot. If the server offers a toothpick, spear the *hors d'oeuvre*, put it in your mouth and then deposit the used toothpick on a plate or receptacle put out for that purpose. If there isn't a toothpick available, hold it in your napkin until you can find a wastebasket. Never put a used toothpick back on the serving tray.

When appetizers have remnants, such as shrimp tails, hold them in a paper napkin until you can dispose of them. Do not discard toothpicks, napkins, uneaten appetizers, or any other food in an ashtray. Besides making a mess, the paper napkins create a fire hazard.

Olives

Eat with your fingers if they are served as a relish. If there are pits, remove the stones with your fingers. Bite a large, stuffed olive in half. Put only small ones in your mouth whole. (When the olive is in a salad, eat it with a fork, not your fingers.)

FIRST COURSES

Artichokes

Tear off a leaf, dip it briefly in the usually accompanying vinaigrette or butter sauce, and pull it through your teeth to remove the edible part. If it is stuffed, spread the stuffing on the leaf with your knife. When you reach the thinner inner leaves, discard them. Cut out the hairy center and you are left with the heart, which is then eaten with knife and fork.

Avocados

When it is served in its skin, hold the shell to steady it with one hand and eat the fruit with a spoon. If it is filled with a salad mixture, you also hold the shell with one hand while eating the contents with a fork. Put your fork on your plate between bites as well as when you are finished. Never leave the fork in the shell.

Caviar

If passed to you in a bowl with its own spoon, serve a spoonful onto your plate. Take small amounts of minced onion, sieved egg whites and yolks, lemon slices, and toast when they are passed to you. Assemble the canapé with your knife, and then pick it up with your hand.

Clams and Oysters on the Half Shell

Hold the shell with the fingers of one hand and hold the shellfish fork with the other hand. Spear the meat with a fork. At formal dinners, sauce is usually not served. If it is, dip it into the sauce and eat it with one bite. Never cut a raw clam or oyster. Only if you are in an informal setting may you sip the liquid from the shell.

For steamed clams, take the fully opened shell (if the shell isn't open, don't eat it) and pull out the neck of the clam with your cocktail fork (if it's a formal dinner). Remove the sheath from around the neck, with your hands and, holding it by this neck, dip the clam into a cup of broth, then in melted butter, and eat it in one bite. Fried clams, oysters, and mussels can be cut with a fork.

Frogs' Legs

These may be eaten with the fingers or with a knife and fork. Disjoint large ones with a knife and fork before picking them up. Move the inedible portions to the side of the plate with your knife and fork.

Mussels

When they are served in their shells in a broth, mussels may be removed from their shells with a fork, dipped into a sauce and eaten in one bite. Empty shells are placed in a specially provided bowl or plate. The remaining juice or broth may be eaten with a spoon or may be sopped up with a piece of bread speared on the tines of your fork.

Shrimp Cocktail

If the shrimp are not impossibly large, they should be eaten in one bite. But when shrimp are of a jumbo size, grasp the cup in which they are served firmly with one hand, and cut the shrimp as neatly as possible with the edge of your fork. If the saucer or plate underneath is large enough, you might remove it from the cup, place it on the saucer and cut it with a knife and fork.

If a lemon wedge is served with the shrimp, spear it with your fork and then, covering the back of the wedge with your other hand, squeeze it carefully over the shrimp. If sauce is served, and the sauce dish is yours alone, you may dip the shrimp into it. If the sauce is to be shared, spoon some of the sauce over the shrimp on your plate. (This applies to any sauce that is served during the meal.)

Snails

Snail shells are grasped with a special holder in one hand or with your fingers, protected with your napkin, if no holder is provided. Remove the meat with a pick or oyster fork held in the other hand. You may pour the garlic butter that remains in the shells onto the snail plate and sop it up with small pieces of French bread on the end of a fork.

Soup

Hold the soup spoon in your right hand with your thumb on top. While eating, tip the spoon slightly away from you and fill it by moving it away from you, not toward you. Sip the soup noiselessly from the side of the spoon.

When most of the soup is eaten, you may tip the plate away, not toward you, to get the last drops. Soup bowls should always be served on a plate so that the soiled spoon can be put on it and not left in the bowl. (At a luncheon or less formal meal, soup may be served in a bouillon-or-cream soup cup and stand, and you may drink it by lifting the cup with your hands.)

Crackers or Croutons with Soup

These are scattered on top of the soup after it has been ladled into the plate and are usually passed by the waiter. Each person may scatter a spoonful directly onto the soup, making sure that the serving spoon doesn't actually touch the soup.

FISH COURSE

To eat fish, one holds the fork in the left hand, tines down, and uses the knife as a cutter and pusher. If the fish is soft and boneless, then it is perfectly proper to use only the fork. When the fork is held in the right hand, the tines may be up or down, whichever is more convenient. If you are eating only with the fork, don't put the knife on the plate. Leave it on the table. And when using only the fork, always hold it in your right hand. Most often, fish is served in fillet form and eaten with a fish fork and knife. If there is no fish knife and fork, use any knife and fork that is in front of you.

If a fish is served whole and you have to fillet it yourself, first cut off the head and tail with a knife and fork and move them to the side of your plate. Insert the tip of the knife against the backbone and slit the fish from head to tail. You can then flip open the fish and slide the backbone out, or lift the top fillet off, eat it, and then remove the backbone. If you find small bones in your mouth when eating fish, push them to the front of your mouth with your tongue, then onto your fork, removing them to the side of your plate.

Sushi and Sashimi

If these, or any other Asian dishes, are served with chopsticks, use them if you feel comfortable using them. Otherwise, resort to your knife and fork.

Small pieces of sushi are eaten whole; larger pieces can be cut by holding the chopsticks together and slicing into the piece with them. If you are helping yourself from a serving platter, remember to use the large ends of the chopsticks, which have not been in your mouth.

MEAT AND POULTRY

Chicken, Turkey, and Other Fowl

At a formal dinner, no part of a bird is eaten with your fingers. Informally, it is permissible to pick up the bones, after most of the meat has been cut off. Never pick up the body.

Chops

At a dinner party, lamb chops must be eaten with a knife and fork. Cut the center or eye of the chop off the bone and then cut the meat into two or three pieces. If the chop has a frilled paper skirt around the end of the bone, you may hold the skirt in your hand and cut the meat from the side of the bone. If there is no skirt, do the best you can with a knife and fork.

STEAK AND ROASTS

The meat knife is not held like the fish knife, because more leverage for cutting is necessary. Point your forefinger down the knife's bridge to steady it. The fork should be in your left hand, with the tines down. Do not hold the fork in your fist and stab the meat with it. Spear the meat with the fork and cut it with the knife. Cut only one piece at a time. To fix the meat onto the fork's tines, put the knife blade underneath the piece of meat. A small amount of potatoes and vegetables may be placed on the tines of the fork with the meat.

Never hold the fork in the left hand with the tines up and pile food on it with a knife.

Never place the knife and fork on your plate like a pair of oars in a rowboat while you are eating. Cross them. This is the only "rest" position. The knife and fork are crossed on the plate with the fork over the knife with the tines facedown.

Don't gesticulate with the knife and fork in your hands. The knife should never be raised more than an inch or two above the plate.

When eating a piece of bread or drinking, place the knife and fork in the rest position. The knife blade's sharp edge should be pointing to the left.

When the course is finished, always place knife and fork parallel to each other on the plate, tines of the fork down. The knife blade should face the fork.

If the meat doesn't require cutting with a knife, it may be eaten with the fork in the right hand. In this case, don't use the knife at all. Leave it on the table. If you are eating the meat with only the fork, place the fork tines facing up on the plate when you are finished.

VEGETABLES

ASPARAGUS

When asparagus is served without a sauce, and the stalks are firm, it is finger food. If it is dripping with hollandaise sauce, eat it with a knife and fork. When in doubt, do what the hostess does. (This is a good rule to follow for just about everything.) In the great houses, asparagus was served with tongs, then picked up by the thick end and dipped in oiled (melted) butter.

CORN

Corn on the cob is not served at formal dinners. If there is to be corn, it is usually cut from the cob in the kitchen before it is served. When you do eat corn on the cob, butter only a few sections at a time, keeping the mess on your face and hands to a minimum. Eat it as quietly as possible.

PEAS

These are perhaps the most difficult vegetable to eat. One method is to use your knife as a pusher to get them onto your fork. Another is to spear a few peas with the tines of your fork.

POTATOES

Baked potatoes, whether white or sweet, are usually split in half with the fingers, cutting a slit with a knife first. Then, mix in the butter, pepper, and salt with a fork. At formal meals, French fries are eaten with a fork.

PASTA

Spaghetti, Linguini, and fettuccini

Take a few strands onto your fork and twirl them around the fork, holding the tines against the edge of your plate. Alternatively, twirl the pasta strands around a large spoon, if one is served. In either case, the strands should be twirled until there are no dangling ends. Bring the fork to your mouth. If the ends do unwind, you must either suck them quietly into your mouth or bite them neatly, hoping they fall back onto your fork, not onto your clothes or plate.

Lasagna and Layered Pasta

When faced with the possibility of melted strings of cheese stretching from the plate to the fork in your mouth, cut your portion with a knife. The best idea is to cut through the cheese first, before attempting to bite into a mouthful.

SALAD

Cut large pieces of lettuce with a fork (or a fork and knife if they are particularly difficult to cut with just a fork). If you think that just the fork will do, leave the knife on the table. Cut only one bite at a time. Use your salad fork if the salad is served on a separate plate. If it comes on your entrée plate, eat it with your entrée fork. At a luncheon, salad is often served at the same time as the meat course. In this case you may use the same fork you are using for the meat.

FRUITS

APPLES

These are quartered with a knife. The core is then cut away and the fruit is eaten with the fingers. If you don't want to eat the skin, pare each quarter separately.

APRICOTS AND PLUMS

Hold these fruits with your fingers and eat them as close to the pit as possible. When you remove a pit with your fingers, you should do it with your thumb underneath the stone and your first two fingers across its top.

BANANAS

When you are dining out, peel the skin all the way off, lay the fruit on your plate, cut it in slices, and eat with a fork.

BERRIES

Before serving, berries are usually hulled or stemmed. When especially fine and freshly picked, strawberries are often served with their hulls on and sugar is placed on the side of each person's plate. Hold the hull with your fingers, dip the fruit into the sugar and then eat it. Discarded hulls should be placed on the side of the plate.

Cantaloupes and Other Melons

When served in halves or quarters, melons are eaten with a spoon. When served in precut pieces, they are eaten with a fork.

Cherries

Cherries are a finger fruit. Drop the cherry pit into your almost closed, cupped hand and then deposit it on your plate.

Figs

If fresh figs are served as an appetizer with prosciutto, they are eaten skin and all with a knife and fork. As a dessert, cut up and covered in a sauce, they are eaten with a fork and spoon. If they are served *au naturel,* halve them and eat them with a knife and fork.

Grapefruit

When this fruit is served, the seeds should have been removed and each section precut and loosened. The rind and any additional seeds should be left on the plate. Grapefruit is eaten with either a teaspoon or a pointed citrus spoon.

Grapes

Never pull one grape at a time off the bunch. Choose a bunch with several grapes on it, and break it off. If grape scissors are provided, cut the bunch off close to the main stem. Grapes with seeds may be put in your mouth whole. Deposit the seeds into your fingers and place them on your plate as elegantly as possible.

KIWIS

These should be peeled and then sliced like a tomato. If you are served an unpeeled one, use a sharp paring knife to strip away the outer skin, then slice the kiwi crosswise.

ORANGES AND TANGERINES

Remove the skin from these citrus fruits by slicing off the two ends of the rind and then cutting the peel into vertical strips. If the peel is loose, you may pry it free with your fingers. Tangerines can be pulled apart into small sections before eating, while oranges are more easily cut with a knife.

Remove seeds with the tip of a knife. Fiber may be removed with fingers. Remove any remaining fiber and seeds from your mouth neatly. Oranges can also be eaten like grapefruit, with a grapefruit spoon or teaspoon, provided they have been precut in half.

PEACHES

These are cut to the pit, then broken in half, quartered, and consumed with a dessert knife and fork. You can remove the skin or eat it.

PEARS

Like apples, these are quartered with a knife. The core is then cut away, and the fruit is eaten with the fingers. But if the pears are very juicy, they should be eaten with a fork.

PINEAPPLE

Pineapple is sliced into round pieces, served on a plate, and eaten with a dessert knife and fork.

PERSIMMONS

Set the fruit upright on the plate, stem-end down, and cut it into quarters, which you open out until they lie flat. Cut each quarter into pieces that can be eaten with a knife and fork. Persimmons can also be cut in half and the meat scooped out with a spoon. Never eat the skin, which tends to be bitter.

POMEGRANATES

This is a fruit in which the meat is discarded and the seeds are eaten. At a dinner party, the pomegranate is usually served halved on a plate. Carefully pick out the seeds with a spoon, steadying the fruit between your index finger and thumb. Suck the flesh off the seeds and discard them.

WATERMELON

At a formal dinner table, use a fork. Remove the seeds with the tines and then cut the pieces with the side of the fork.

DESSERTS

The general rule is this: If you cannot eat something without getting it all over your fingers and face, use a fork, and, when necessary, a spoon or knife as well. Dessert may be eaten with the fork in the left hand (tines down) and the spoon in the right. Eat with the spoon. The fork only serves as the pusher. If you are eating pie or cake, only the fork need be used. If it is ice cream, pudding, or zabaglione, use the spoon. The other piece of flatware is left on the table.

While you are eating, you employ the same "rest" position with the fork and spoon as the one you used for the knife and fork during the meat course. The fork tines should be facing downward, lying over the spoon. When you are finished, the flatware is again placed parallel on the plate with the fork tines down and the spoon bowl up. If dessert is served in a stemmed glass on a service plate, the spoon is placed on the service plate, never left in the glass, even while eating. If dessert is in a dish that resembles a soup plate or sauce dish, leave the spoon in the dish or put it on the service plate if there is enough room.

Dessert Cheese
In the United States, these cheeses are usually served with fruit. Eat the cheese with a fork and the fruit with either a fork or the fingers. In England they are only served with biscuits.

Layer Cake
Slices should always be placed on their side on a dessert plate, not standing up because it is almost impossible to cut cake neatly when it is upright. If it is served to you standing up, turn the slice on its side with your dessert fork and spoon.

PASTRIES

Confections such as cream puffs and Napoleons are held down with the dessert spoon and cut and eaten with the dessert fork. Bite-sized pastries may be eaten with your fingers.

PIE

Cakes and pies are eaten with a fork. If the dessert is served *à la mode*, a spoon is also used. Ice cream is generally eaten with a spoon but when accompanied by cake, either the spoon, or the fork and spoon may be used.

STEWED FRUIT

Hold it in place with the fork, and cut and eat it with a spoon.

CANDY AND PETIT FOURS

When these are presented on a serving platter in paper wrappers or cups, lift them from the serving dish in their paper. Do not leave the paper on the serving dish.

All of this knowledge I've shared in the book, of course, must also be accompanied with grace and assurance, so that even if you do make a mistake, no one will think ill of you. I remember when I worked as a footman at West Wycombe Park in Buckinghamshire in 1932 and the then Duchess of York (the future queen mother) came to tea. We were serving early greenhouse strawberries in May. On the table were bowls of sugar in casters as well as large, glass salt cellars containing very fine salt, which looked like sugar.

Whilst taking the strawberries around to the guests, I noticed the Duchess helping herself to cream and what she thought was sugar from the large glass salt cellars. Before I could get back to warn her, she had dipped a luscious strawberry in the cream and salt and taken a bite.

Her grace, in her usual charming manner, made little of this incident. I must say I admired her handling of the situation and thought what a gracious lady she was.

Winston Churchill, on the other hand, was a nightmare to work for. When I was employed at Blenheim Palace, if his valet was away, I had to take over. He would keep his dinner guests up talking when the staff had to be up again at 6:30 A.M. We would consider ourselves lucky if we could get into the dining room to clear before midnight. Then he would stay in bed until midday, constantly ringing his wretched bell. And such trivial things! A cup of tea or to pick up a paper that had fallen off his bed! He was a right handful.

But most of the famous people I have served were true ladies and gentlemen. And alas, we shall never see the likes of these days in private service again. All the knowledge that I've accumulated over the years is not being passed on, so when I and a few other prewar-trained domestic staff pass on there will be none to take over and carry on the traditions of three to four hundred years of the science of domestic service.

I hope that this book will in some small way help to remedy that. To see my book in print has fulfilled a long-felt ambition of mine. I have enjoyed my contribution to the art of gracious living and hope I have been able to bring some small part of it alive for you.

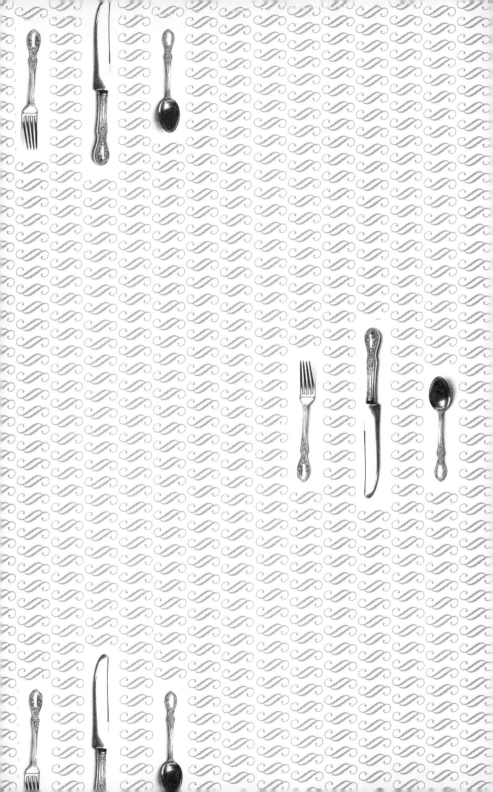

ARTHUR INCH'S GUIDE
TO THE HIERARCHY OF MENSERVANTS IN THE 18TH, 19TH, AND 20TH CENTURIES, AND THEIR DUTIES

STEWARD

He controlled the household, paid all the accounts and supervised all the staff. I knew of only one during the '30s.

BUTLER

He became the head of the household after the post of steward died out. He was the head of the staff. He supervised all the menservants. The housekeeper was in charge of the housemaids and still room (smaller kitchen) maids, and the chef/cook was in charge of all the kitchen staff, but the butler was in charge overall. Any disputes among the staff were sorted out by him before appealing to the master or mistress of the house

A butler—and this also applies to all menservants—had to be clean shaven with a short, neat haircut. You never saw a butler with a mustache or a beard. He would be quiet and dignified and keep a firm hand on the menservants and would be addressed as "sir" by the menservants and "mister" by the rest of the staff. In Edwardian times, he would dress in a black morning coat, black waistcoat, and striped trousers with either a high, stiff collar or a wing collar, and either a black tie or bow. He would always put on a short black jacket for luncheon and then in the evening would change into evening dress.

If no valet was kept, the butler would assume the duties of a butler/valet and look after the master's clothes. He was responsible for the wine cellar and kept a wine-cellar book to record all incoming wine and delete the wine drunk. He would be responsible for laying down the wine in the old store bins, helped by the odd man who finished suitable lengths of battens to put between the rows of bottles. He also selected the wines for dinner.

If married, he and his family would live in a cottage nearby but he would always have a bedroom in the house where he changed his clothes or slept over in the case of a late party.

GROOM OF CHAMBERS

He was next in command to the butler and, should the butler be absent for any reason, the groom of chambers took command. In early times, he was actually what the name implies, a man in charge of the chambers or public rooms, a sort of super houseman in charge of all the furniture, drapes, antiques, etc. But latterly, he attended to all the writing tables in public rooms, making sure there was an adequate supply of headed notepaper and that the inkwells were topped up with ink and that there were plenty of pens and pencils on hand.

He also received and dispatched all the mail and made sure all letters were adequately stamped, etc. He was responsible for ordering all the newspapers and periodicals and making sure the newspapers were ironed (yes, they ironed newspapers!) and folded properly before being placed on the ladies' breakfast trays and taken upstairs. In the absence of the butler, he would assume command. (I worked with only one, at Blenheim Palace, and I shouldn't think there is one left now, with the exception of the royal residences.)

VALET

He was the personal servant to the master of the house and looked after all his clothing and shoes. He occasionally helped at large dinner parties, and if no groom of chambers was kept, he would take charge if the butler was absent.

UNDERBUTLER

He was in charge of and responsible for the silver safe and the cleaning and polishing of all the silver, both in the safe and the public rooms. He had a pantry boy to help with the pantry work. His special duty was the laying up of the dinner table, and he was also responsible for bringing each course to the dining room from the kitchen. He helped serve the dinner at the table. He had to check and put away all the silver after the dinner party and make sure it was locked up in the safe. He wore the same livery as the footmen.

FOOTMAN

In earlier days he was what the name implied, a "foot soldier," and was used as a guard in the carriage. Two footmen would stand at the back of the carriage. Each carried long pointed staves and, in more lawless days, used to beat off footpads (highwaymen) who were trying to molest the passengers. In early Georgian and Victorian days there might be as many as six to eight footmen in the large stately homes, but in my days in the '30s, we usually had three footmen. In smaller houses this would be reduced to two and sometimes one.

The footmen laid up all the dining room meals except the dinner table. They also had to answer all bells (i.e., calls for service), and if not on duty, they had to do some silver cleaning. They acted as a valet to any younger male member of the family or any male guests who did not bring their own valets.

Like the butler, they would be cleanshaven. They would be dressed in a white starched front and cuffs, a shirt with a wing collar and a white bow tie. They would wear black box-cloth trousers and a horizontally striped waistcoat in the colors of the master's coat of arms. Their tailcoat could be black, dark blue, brown, or maroon, with about twenty-eight silver-plated or brass buttons embossed with the family crest. (These had to be cleaned every day.) Fingernails had to be kept short and clean. (The butler would check.)

If only two footmen were kept, the first footman would wear livery all day to answer bells or the front door. He would also lay meals and wait luncheon and dinner. He was also the lady's footman and kept all her downstairs coats brushed and all the shoes cleaned. If she were a hunting lady, he would have the riding and hunting habits to keep clean as well as keeping her hunting boots polished. The second footman would be dressed in working clothes during the morning and would be responsible for keeping all the silver cleaned and getting all the silver required for luncheon and dinner and help with the laying of the table. He would change into his footman's livery to help with luncheon and dinner and, with the first footman, would take the tea into the dining room. A footman would wear cotton gloves to serve dinner.

STEWARD'S OR HOUSEKEEPER'S ROOM BOY

He laid up the table for meals in the head servant's room, known as the Pugs' Parlour, served them, and then cleaned up and washed up all the utensils. Sometimes, at big parties, he also had to lend a hand in the pantry.

HALL BOY

He looked after all the under servants' meals in the servants' hall (the under butler was head here). He brought in all the meals and had to clean and wash up later. He also kept the hall clean and tidy, sweeping out and mopping up the floor and wiping down tables and sideboards. In wintertime, he was in charge of lighting the fire.

It was his job to clean all the cutlery and see to laying the hall table for all meals. For dinner and supper, he would collect a pile of hot plates from the kitchen and then place the main meat dish in front of the butler, who would serve out the portions, which would then be passed around the table. He would have placed the dishes of hot vegetables on the table and the staff would help themselves.

Beginning in 1905, it was his job to put jugs of beer on the table for anyone who wanted it and probably cider for female staff. After the first course had been cleared, he would place the pudding and plates in front of the housekeeper at the other end of the table for her to serve the portions. In some places the head servants would take their pudding into the housekeeper's room. The hall boy then cleaned the table and washed up all the cutlery. (The plates were washed up by the scullery maid.) Sometimes, at big dining room parties, he would be required to help the odd man run the dinner from the kitchen to the dining room and wash up in the butler's pantry. The hall boy dressed in a working suit, usually a dark tweed.

PANTRY BOY

He helped the under butler clean silver and also had to keep the pantry clean, scrubbing the table, sideboards, floor, etc.

ODD MAN

He looked after the two large, coke-fired boilers in the basement that supplied the central heating as well as the smaller boiler that heated all the household water. He also carried coal up to the various landings for the housemaids to use in the bedroom fires. He chopped the kindling wood for the housemaids for laying their fires and also filled all the log baskets in the front rooms.

When visiting gentry came to stay he would collect the luggage and take it up to their rooms. He also swept and cleaned the back passages and did any other odd job that cropped up, including helping to serve at large dinner parties.

GLOSSARY OF TERMS

ASHETTE AND COVER A big oval dish for serving roasts.

BAIZE A coarse woolen or cotton fabric, usually green, napped to imitate felt.

BOX CLOTH A heavy wool that was originally used for the footman's livery when he had to guard the carriage (the carriage is the "box") and stand outside of it. The term continued to be used even when people had switched from horses to cars.

CARTRIDGE PAPER Heavy white paper used for lining drawers, so named because it was originally used to stuff pellets down cartridges. Once, when my mother was sent to get some cartridge paper from the stationers, she forgot its name and asked for shooting paper.

CASTER A container used for caster sugar, which is simply a very fine sugar whose grains are small enough to flow through the sprinkler holes atop the caster. In the United States it is sold as very fine sugar.

CLARET — Another name for Bordeaux wines.

FOOTPAD — A robber, a highwayman.

LIVERY — It stands for *what is delivered*: the clothes of a manservant, delivered to him by his master, are his livery. It is also defined as the distinctive clothing or badge worn by retainers of a person of rank.

MITER FOLDS — A miter (spelled mitre in England) is the headdress worn by bishops and abbots. A miter-folded napkin copies the profile.

NAPERY — Household linens, especially table linen.

PUDDING — The generic term for sweets such as crème brulée or ice cream.

RUNNING THE DINNER — Bringing the dinner from the kitchen to the dining room.

ROUGE — A red powder consisting essentially of ferric oxide used for polishing glass, metal, or gems and as a pigment.

SAVORIES

Savories (spelled savouries in the U.K.) are tangy and in early twentieth-century England were traditionally served after sweets as a sort of palate cleanser prior to the service of after-dinner drinks. Today, the term most often refers to tidbits served as appetizers, or to more substantial dishes that can be served for lunch: quiches, tarts, vol au vents, and timbales, for example.

SCULLERY MAID

A servant whose chief task is washing dishes, pots, pans, and vegetables.

STILL ROOM

The second kitchen, where bread, cakes, and jams were made and fruits were bottled. It was smaller than the main kitchen where the meals were cooked. (In *Gosford Park* there was a still room maid.) In large houses there were usually two head maids and an undermaid.

TEA SERVICE

This consisted of a two-handled silver tray with a silver kettle on a stand that had a mentholated spirit burner underneath to keep the boiling water hot when taken up to the drawing room. It also included a silver teapot, sugar basin, and milk jug. It was placed on a table that was covered with a lovely tea cloth and used with a china service of cups, saucers, and plates. Napkins were never used at teatime.

TRINITY
VEGETABLE DISH

A round silver dish with a cover and removable black handle. Inside is a three-division removable section to keep three kinds of vegetables separate.

WHITING

Calcium carbonate prepared as a fine powder by grinding and washing, used especially as a pigment or extender in putty and in rubber compounding and paper coating. It was used to clean silver instead of plate powder or rouge.

BIBLIOGRAPHY

Baldridge, Laetitia. *The Amy Vanderbilt Complete Book of Etiquette*, revised and expanded by Letitia Baldridge. New York: Doubleday, 1978.

Hirst, Arlene. *Every Woman's Guide to China, Glass and Silver.* New York: Arco, 1970.

Hoving, Walter. *Tiffany's Table Manners for Teenagers.* New York: Random House, 1989.

Inch, Arthur Richard. *Reminiscences of a Life in Private Service.* London: Trinity Press, 1998.

Martin, Judith. *Miss Manners' Guide for the Turn of the Millennium.* New York: Simon and Schuster, Fireside Editions, 1990.

Meyer, Sylvia, et al., translated by Heinz Holtmann. *Professional Table Service.* New York: John Wiley & Sons, 1991.

Mitchell, Mary, with John Corr. *The Complete Idiot's Guide to Etiquette*, Second Edition. New York: Alpha Books, 2000.

Post, Emily, and Peggy Post. *Emily Post's Etiquette* (16th Edition). New York: Harper Collins, 1997.

Post, Peggy. *Emily Post's Essentials: Everyday Etiquette.* New York: Harper Paperbacks, 1999.

Segaloff, Nat. *The Everything Etiquette Book.* Avon, Massachusetts: Adams Media Corporation, 1998.

Taylor, Lynn Claire. *The Etiquette of Etiquette.* Layton, Utah: Gibbs Smith, 2002.

Tuckerman, Nancy, and Nancy Dunnan. *The Amy Vanderbilt Complete Book of Etiquette, 50th Anniversary Edition.* New York: Doubleday, 1995.

Udell, Rochelle. *How to Eat an Artichoke.* New York: G.P. Putnam's Sons, 1982.

Von Drachenfels, Suzanne. *The Art of the Table.* New York: Simon and Schuster, 2000.

WEBSITES

all-about-fabrics.com
askyahoo.com
bizforum.org/etiquette.htm
caplanduval.com
epicurious. com
hintsandthings.co.uk
soyouwanna.com

**Flatware, china, and glassware illustrations
courtesy of Replacements, Ltd.**
www.replacements.com